Goodbye White Rose

Gina Azizah

Copyright © 2024 Gina Azizah

The moral right of the author has been asserted.

Apart from any fair dealing for the purposes of research or private study, or criticism or review, as permitted under the Copyright, Designs and Patents Act 1988, this publication may only be reproduced, stored or transmitted, in any form or by any means, with the prior permission in writing of the publishers, or in the case of reprographic reproduction in accordance with the terms of licences issued by the Copyright Licensing Agency. Enquiries concerning reproduction outside those terms should be sent to the publishers.

Matador
Unit E2 Airfield Business Park,
Harrison Road, Market Harborough,
Leicestershire. LE16 7UL
Tel: 0116 2792299
Email: books@troubador.co.uk
Web: www.troubador.co.uk/matador
Twitter: @matadorbooks

ISBN 978 1805142 058

British Library Cataloguing in Publication Data.
A catalogue record for this book is available from the British Library.

Printed and bound in the UK by TJ Books Limited, Padstow, Cornwall
Typeset in 11pt Minion Pro by Troubador Publishing Ltd, Leicester, UK

Matador is an imprint of Troubador Publishing Ltd

Country Girl

Harisun Binti Isa is my mum's name; she was born in the countryside. And my mum's birth took place on 4 December 1945. My mum didn't tell me anything about when she was a baby, but she did tell me about when she was growing up as a young girl. My mum came from the countryside so she was just a very normal country girl with a very simple life, but life for her was like a beautiful dream. My mum had nothing: no toys to play with, no friend to run around with, only keeping herself busy listening to the birds singing; that was the biggest treasure in the world for her. Also the simple life didn't stop my mum from having fun and being joyful on her own; in fact it kept her busy, connecting herself with the natural world. All those things made my mum so happy, the simple things in life.

I am so proud of my mum, even at very young age she was very mature, like a grown woman who looked after her mother's responsibilities seriously. Sometimes life was not so easy for my mum, but at a young age she learned things in life. For my mum her simple life was a circle of happiness, sadness, hard times and good times; however, she went through more hard times than good times. Well, that is all life is about: it was painful for my mum when she had hard times but she was sometimes full of happiness when she had beautiful times. One afternoon my mum thought to live a simple life with a simple plan, so she could continue to enjoy her life and make each day count, always finding peacefulness in the countryside where she belongs.

With her long black hair with a glorious smile and her high cheekbones, of course my mum was a beautiful woman. My mum was very talkative with her beautiful smile; she would talk to everyone she met. At that time in the countryside my mum didn't know about fashion or make-up. Coming from the countryside, also as a Muslim, my mum was not allowed to wear trousers, a skirt or to put on make-up. Every day my mum wore a sarong and a long loose shirt or a traditional Malay dress with a fully covered-up head. Luckily at that time my mum had no need to cover her head or wear the hijab. Good for my mum because her character was just like a boy's: never staying at home, running around everywhere.

My mum's parents worked as rubber tappers, so she was always out in the jungle surrounded by the rubber trees. Rubber trees are beautiful; in fact, I too grew up exactly like my mum, as a country girl with a very simple life. I never did the work, but I saw my mum use the tapper. I remember my mum waking up in the early hours to do the tapper so the tree would bring more milk and my mum could get more money.

One day at about four in the morning my mum asked me to follow her. I was so tired and sleepy but at the same time was so excited to see how my mum did the rubber tapper. The morning was so calm and silent, only hearing our footsteps. I was still at a very young age, following my mum's back with my hand grabbing her clothes, so scared, but if anything happened I would run off safe myself. My mum went from one tree to another; at the beginning I did not concentrate. My mind and my eyes were busy looking around in the dark in case anything popped up, errr… I had goosebumps. But my mum was so brave. With a fire lamp tied around her head she worked so fast without worrying about anything. After I became a little confident I watched my mum doing the tapper. My mum tapped the thick and soft plant bark with a rubber carving knife to take latex for the job. Then I could see the white blood dripping from the cross mark into the tub for my mum to collect it into a bucket later as latex. That was the first and last time I saw how my mum did the rubber tapper – never again.

Anyway, the winds blew between the rubber trees and my mum faced the glory of the afternoon breeze. As she was a country girl, my mum just wore a sarong and shirt; however, she still managed to climb the tree better than the monkey. My mum was a bird lover; as a bird lover she always searched for the perfect nesting spot in the tree. As soon as my mum found one she would climb the tree to look at the tiny birdie. Every day my mum would return to the nesting spot and stand there looking at the birdie, listening to the birdie cry – it would sound like a musical. Most of the time my mum would gather food daily for the birdie and tenderly feed them, hand to beak. What was the most wonderful thing was the way my mum cared for the birdie – absolutely splendid and unique. The crying of the birdie gave my mum something so joyful and entertaining to her soul. But then the time came when all the birdies grew big and their wings were strong enough to take them to fly up and be gone. They left my mum all alone with the empty nests.

The flowing branches of the trees prevented the sun from touching the earth; that is nature. Also as my mum is a downright country girl, her soul full of pride, she loves to swim in the river. In fact, she is a very good swimmer. Sometimes my mum swam and swam nonstop like she was swimming for her life. Even on a hot, sunny day my mum didn't care about the sun; luckily she had dark skin. For my mum swimming was fun; it brought so much happiness and reaching for her life. My mum never got enough of swimming or tired of swimming, and sometimes she raced on her own. My mum's arms would splash, splash, splash, the waves splashing, crashing. She would not even hear the noises she'd make and she would not even know how fast a speed she swam. After my mum had enough of swimming then my mum would jump and swim deep in the water; suddenly she would come out with a fish in her hand. Then my mum would swim again to get more fish, and those fish she would bring back home for her mother to cook for their meals. My mum became like a crazy fisherman, catching it with a hook. She was brilliant at catching the fish. After my mum had enough of catching the fish she then relaxed in the water with her heart to the river. The river looked so calm, but my mum was on her own with so much happiness, giving all her love to the river. The sound of the running water made my mum's brain so peaceful, especially hearing the birds sing in the trees. It was a splendid time that she had on her own in the river. My mum then laid floating while her eyes looked up at the blue sky, moving clouds and the smiling sun, a natural creation, absolutely a beauty. My mum admired the amazing river keeping on flowing, but then she felt the cold in her bones. Without thinking twice my mum drank the river water from her hand that came from the mountain of love – clean, fresh. Slowly my mum took her last lungful and lowered her head gently, going with the flow. My mum then took her time sitting in the river, watching water dancing around in the river, pure and clean, feeling like she was in heaven. Her mind was thinking about the beauty of nature and life created by God in this planet earth bringing gloriousness into her life. These memories of my mum's childhood will stay with her for the rest of her life. Especially the surroundings: rubber trees, the greenness and mountain – it was breathtaking.

My mum felt her life shared more with nature than humans, which she enjoyed very much. Especially in the early morning, my mum would rush to the jungle when all the trees and nature start to wake up. Standing on her own surrounded all around with nature, my mum would keep breathing the fresh clean air, full of oxygen – it just brought her heart so much happiness. To smell the wildflowers surrounding the jungle brought her spirit and soul back to life. She would look at the brown leaves on the trees starting to change to green; this is a miracle from heaven.

My mum heard nonstop the birds speaking their own language, which made her smile, full of happiness. Slowly my mum would look up at the blue sky thinking what a beautiful colour – there is so much nature in this planet that we can appreciate. Then gently my mum would close her eyes, whispering in her heart, 'I can't think anything better than taking advantage of this perfect time in nature.'

Life was something that my mum always looked forward to because every second you move life can change to another step of life. Whatever my mum had in life, she was blessed and thanked God for letting her stay on this beautiful planet earth. My mum's life could sometimes be very boring because she kept herself to herself, and all her sadness she kept in silence. It could be very depressing, but that was who she was; she couldn't change herself. Most of the time my mum settled her problems on her own and went on with life, keeping her smile and being happy. What my mum always loved to do was wander alone to see another thing in the jungle that filled her with surprise, that made her forget everything. Sometimes my mum sat by the river for hours to see the water in the river attracting many kinds of fish, swimming happily and chasing one another – absolutely beautiful. And all the trees were alive, fluttering and waving as the breeze came along, making her day so glorious. My mum always noticed when the day started to brighten; it brought all the birds in jungle to life happily. Then when the sun went down some of the insects start to wake up at night. All this made my mum so excited to learn even more about the beauty of natural creations from God.

As my mum came from a big family life was hard for her mother, especially as her father had a second wife and most of the time he spent his time with his second wife. Isa was my mum; her father left his wife Patema, my mum's mother, for a few months without taking responsibility for his family. So this left Patema in difficulty – finding her daily basics to put food on the table and to feed all her children. She thanked God for my mum; at her young age she already understood her mother's hard life. That is the reason my mother spent her time – almost the whole day, every day – doing lots of things in the jungle. Also as a country girl, the jungle is the place for my mum to enjoy her time. Especially as my mum appreciated nature and loved animals – it was perfect for her. Amazingly my mum could walk barefoot, running and crawling through the jungle – phew! I don't how she managed running barefoot. The most funny thing my mum did was follow the monkeys dancing from the tree to tree while she was on the ground – that was hilarious. At the same time my mum talked to the monkey and said, 'Hey! Monkey, you are so happy, swinging free from tree to tree, and cheeky to throw a leaf at me.'

The monkey looked at my mum with her smiling face and her hair wildly curly, hanging by his hands and feet in case my mum had a treat for him to eat, but my mum said again, 'Hey! Monkey, come down and play with me.' The monkey didn't bother with whatever my mum said, instead continuing to swing through the trees. With a happy smile my mum looked at the monkey which made her feel good every day.

Honestly my mum's mind was overgrown in the jungle because she didn't know anything about what happened on the other side of the world. In fact my mum lived with her world surrounded by nature, enjoying her space. Anyway, after my mum caught a few fish she then went to collect some vegetables or mushrooms. My mum learnt a lot of things in the jungle; obviously she knew the kinds of vegetable that she could eat and the kinds of mushroom that would poison you. Then my mum would go to search some woods for her mother to make a wood-fired stove to cook all their meals, because at that time my mum's house had no electricity. Somehow for my mum everything she did was connected with the ground – it was kind of fun, especially to make her mother happy. After my mum did everything her mother needed she then put fish and vegetables in the sack. And then my mum tied up all the wood together properly, then she held the wood over her head. With so much happiness in my mum's heart she just couldn't wait to go home and tell her mother about how great she was with all that stuff. My mum walked back home, with her slippers full of mud, along the pathway while the sun prolonged the shadow of the mountains. The happiness made my mum sing a little happy song, and she hopped a little but carefully, with the wood over her head and also a heavy sack in her hand. All the way walking home from the jungle my mum heard the evening wind say goodbye while the sleeping sunset looked at her with a smile, my mum whispering in her soul, 'Have a good rest, nature, see you again tomorrow.'

As soon my mum arrived home she saw her mother waiting for her. With a smile my mum said, 'Hello, Mum!' She couldn't wait to tell her mum what she'd brought.

With a big smile, and also concern about my mum, her mother said, 'Why have you come home so late? I am so worried about you.'

My mum reply, 'Don't worry, Mum, look what I got for you for our meals.' My mum was so excited to open the sack.

Soon her mother saw all the stuff that my mum brought; her eyes drooped with sadness and happiness. At the same time she said, 'Thank you so much, without you life is nothing, but we've got food until tomorrow.'

My mum was so happy to hear those words she replied, 'For me to eat too, and tomorrow I am going to get more food for us.'

My mum was a very strong character and a wonderful daughter to her mother, who always cared for and always protected her mother. The way my mum did her duty to help her mother is pretty rare. Every day and every hour was so special in her life, and her mother could always count on her. Every day before my mum left the house to go the jungle to search for their daily basics she would do the housework, cleaning, washing everything round the house. My mum was still a young girl, but instead of playing with friends she chose to help her mother. My mum never sat around doing nothing; she never got tired but just wondered how she found the energy. God blessed my mum with an angel because she always understood about life and how difficult it was for her mother to go through life with her father, who always left them and stayed with a second wife. Each time her mother asked for help, my mum would never say no; she would spread her joy and happiness. There were all my mum's brothers and sister; but she was the only one who had a very special bond with her mother like the gift of life. My mum and my grandmother had pretty smiles and both of them had hearts as pure as gold. I am pretty sure my grandmother thanked God that she had such a wonderful daughter who guided her the best she could. One afternoon, full of sunshine around, so bright and so calm, my mum thought how lucky she was to have a mother like an angel. And I was so blessed to have the most precious mother in all the world.

Broken Heart

One day as always every morning my mum woke up very early to help her mother doing the housework. But that day her mother was still in bed which made my mum feel a bit strange because usually her mother woke up early, before anybody else. Well! My mum didn't think much; in fact she continued doing everything around the house. All of a sudden her mother with a crying voice called her for help. My mum was outside the house but soon she heard her mother's voice; she threw everything that was in her hand and rushed like a rocket to see her mother, knowing that her mother was pregnant and time was coming for her mother to give birth. Seeing her mother crying in pain she was scared to leave her, but my mum had to find the midwife while her siblings were around her mother. My mum's father was with his second wife but my mum's older brother was going to find him. On the way to get the midwife my mum thought another sister or brother would be one of the greatest gifts from God, but this time she hadn't prepared or got too excited. Because my mum already had five siblings and the youngest was her brother, who was a year old. And her mother had already been through so much in life. Sometimes my mum would feel a little down because her mother never stopped having babies; it seemed like the pregnancies would never be over. And any moment now another life growing in her mum's womb would be out soon to say hello to the world. Even though my mum was not looking forward to meeting her little sister or brother, she would always feel honoured and privileged to have the little precious thing in her life. From now my mum would be strong, and she closed her eyes and prayed to God for her mother to bring the tiny angel safely into the world.

Anyway, my mum returned home with the midwife then my mum stayed outside the house waiting around to hear the first cry of the little angel. After a few minutes my mum saw her brother walking together with her father; without any word her father went straight inside the house. But my mum looked at her father and thought her father was such an idiot to only come home just to make a baby, with no responsibility to the family.

However my mum enjoyed the glorious morning watching the sunshine smiling down at her and shining from a big bright sky. With a smile my mum whispered to her soul, 'Good morning to the most beautiful world, and the most wonderful start of my day.' Every day brought my mum so much more to look forward to, going to the jungle, but today in this moment it brought her so much delight just being near her mother. Suddenly the birds chirped, which made my mum smile, and that beautiful smile had more radiance than the sun. The only thing was my mum's concern and her hoping everything was going to be fine with her mother. At that moment my mum's day was still excellent, with her heart keeping a smile while her lips made a tiny movement to sing a song. This glorious morning, the sun overhead was shining bright, but for my mum at the moment her day was incomplete without talking to her mother. My mum felt like waiting for her mother to giving birth was like another journey and a day full of a promise to herself to start a new day. What a morning for my mum, especially to see the ground freshly awake, its ray touching everything on the earth. Every morning and every day my mum brings in a new day for her mother, especially with all the foods that she brings from the jungle – they make her mother more radiant. The first thing in the morning when my mum opens her eyes, she thinks about finding the foods for their daily basics, them spreading love and joy for her mother. And for her mother, each morning she was without worry and pain because my mum made sure that her mother was happy every single day. And my mum made sure her mother looked more beautiful than she had yesterday.

The colours of sunrise seemed to fade away suddenly; my mum heard the first cry of the little angel born into the world. It brought a huge smile to my mum's face. With a few birds chirping, making a beautiful melody, and the sound of the baby crying, these made such extraordinary music of nature and the gift of life. With happiness my mum said, 'Yessss! The day is fast and the long wait is finally over – surely the precious gift from God is about to be wrapped.' But then my mum thought of her poor mother, in pain minute by minute and hour by hour as labour progressed.

My mum was so excited to meet the newborn baby, but she would have to wait until everything was ready, and her father would call her and her siblings. While my mum waited to hear her name be called her heart was pumping with happiness and joy, excited to see her mother after feeling relief at her bringing out the baby. The morning sun started to get warm; my mum looked at the sky and she thought she'd never seen the sky so blue. The wind was blowing so calmly, making the trees romantically move around like a slow dance. But my mum's mind was thinking about her mother; she hoped everything that her mother had just gone through was all fine. Without notice tears of deep worry were brought to my mum's eyes and she looked at the ground, the soil that Mother Earth wears, and she felt something was not right. Suddenly my mum heard her father deep male voice calling her name: 'Harisun, come inside to see your baby sister.'

My mum whispered to herself, 'Oh! On the first cry I hear that it's a girl.' When my mum heard the words baby sister she was smiling with joy – such a pleasure to have a baby sister in her life. With small laughter and happiness in my mum's heart, she said it was one of the greatest joys on earth that she would ever know. A day full of sunshine, it was fun for my mum to spend a few glad hours and the greatest happiness in my mum's life to welcome her baby sister to the world. And my mum thought this was one of the reasons why the sky was so blue because a girl brings the most beautiful miracles in life. For sure for my mum life is miracles, and life had changed: another new family member had arrived. For my mum babies are amusing by nature, but for her mother she had a more difficult and stressful life. Because my mum's younger brother was just a year old, and especially because her father would not be around to take responsibility.

Anyway, my mum felt full of butterflies in her stomach; she then quickly ran inside the house to meet the baby girl and her mother. My mum was so excited but her heart stopped; soon she saw everyone surrounding her mother was crying. Slowly my mum walked closer and sat right beside her mother, and this time my mum knew that she would never see her mother again, forever. Her mother had passed away giving birth to her baby sister at the time that my mother was just twelve years old. My mum looked at her new baby sister keeping open a tiny mouth then smiling – so adorable. It was the greatest feeling; my mum couldn't describe it. With sadness, my mum whispered in her heart, 'Welcome to the world, little sister.' Then she prayed to the lord for her baby sister's guidance, and to bring a good family and a good life. As much as my mum loved her baby sister, she already knew that, losing her mother, the road ahead of her was going to be tough. Especially as my mum already had her one-year-old brother for her to take responsibility for, and that was a tremendous burden for her.

Anyway, my mum looked at her mother's face and asked God why her mother's life had been taken so young when she was so beautiful; she wasn't prepared for her to go so soon. Filled with tears for my mum, with a broken heart, gently my mum took her mother's hand and massaged every single finger. It was so hard for my mum to accept that her mother was gone. Losing her mother was one of the hardest things for my mum to go through in life, especially as my mum was just a young girl. Suddenly the sun went pale and the whole world collapsed for my mum.

My mum's mind was full thinking about how she was going to live without her mother in her life and how to say goodbye after so many years with her mother. Just a few hours ago my mum had spoken with her mother and she had asked my mum for help to get the midwife. My mum never expected that help would be the last she would help her mother, and that she would not hear her mother's voice anymore; it broke my mum's heart badly. She did not even have a chance to say a final goodbye, but my mum understood that her mother had struggled and fought for her life until it had come to its end. My mum knew that in a few hours her mother body was going to buried and soon her mother would no longer be with her but would belong to the earth. So time was closing in for my mum to be with her mother; she then started to massage between every one of her mother toes and nonstop kissing those beautiful toes. My mum thought if she could bring her mother's life back she would, but she knew God loved her mother more than she did. Tears ran down my mum's cheeks and her soul comforted her, saying that heaven had chosen to give her mother wings and it was time for her mother to fly. Without a doubt my mum had started to feel all alone, her whole body weak and so low. This was because life had taken away someone so precious; however my mum would try to keep strong, especially for her little one-year-old brother. But then, when my mum looked at her last view of her mother face before she was taken away, my mum's heart whispered, 'Mother, why didn't you say goodbye before you left me.' My poor mum; she thought that her mother was only giving birth, but then it was even worse soon, as she found out that her mother had gone before she knew. Only God knew how many pieces her heart had broken into because a million times my mum needed her at this stage of her life. And a million times my mum's heart was screaming and begging for her to have her mother back. But the miracle would not happen for my mum; her mother's spirit and soul was still taken away, and my mum was left behind without energy.

To say goodbye, words cannot describe the loss my mother felt – of course she knew it was going to be painfully hard and long, but sadly, she was utterly on her own. For the last time before they took her mother's body away my mum took a little precious time and whispered as she closed the book of the journey of her mother's life, saying, 'I love you forever and see you in heaven.'

To see the people taking her mother's body was the hardest time in my mum's life; it was the most painful thing that she ever had experienced. My mum then stood by the window with her one-year-old brother to look at last view with her heart bleeding because without warning her mother had left her. Tears kept dropping on my mum's dress; she couldn't count how much she'd cried, leaving her all shattered and sad. My mum's little brother was smiling and laughing; obviously he didn't understand what was going on at that moment. At such a young age my mum already knew how to play her part for her little brother, putting herself back together and hiding the pain then smiling back at her little brother. My mum tried to be strong, looking at the view with suffering and pain and despairing. Then her whole world came crashing down. With silent tears left and with my mum's heart split in two, she thought her mother was her heart and was the key to her life. But this life had been unfair, taking her mother from her; it was really damaging to her life and left my mum crying in vain.

After they buried her mother my mum was still thinking and found it hard to believe; it was too soon for her mother to be taken from her. How my mum wished she could have just had more time to spend life with her mother, but she had to accept that this was life. Living without her mother of course was the hardest part of my mum's life, but when her mother was alive she did so many things for her. Her mother taught my mum about life, how to survive and how to be independent, and now she knew what to do without her mother. All those special years her mother did the best for my mum, so my mum will do her very best to accept the loss and carry on her life without her mother. With a kind heart, so true, my mum thought her mother deserved a good place in heaven.

Obviously, those special years would not return, with my mum together with her mother, but with the love in my mum's heart surely her mother would walk with her forever. Her mother had been buried for just over an hour, but my mum started to think so many things in her head, especially of her mother's smile, making her life so peaceful. The minutes and hours passed and my mum kept thinking her life would go on without her mother but nothing was the same. As they were from the countryside and my mum was a country girl they never expressed how much they loved each other. Here my mum, all alone, talked to her mother's spirit, said that she loved her mother more than she would ever know. And her mother would be in her heart forever until the day she died. There was too much sadness in my mum's heart because the love that she had for her mother all this time was buried in her mind. My mum only expressed her love to her mother by going in the jungle to find everything that her mother needed. Suddenly silent tears warmly fell down my mum's cheeks and sadly, a few hours after her mother had gone, she still shed tears. No words could describe how empty my mum's heart was because she couldn't talk to and couldn't see her mother for the rest of her life. From this moment my mum stopped smiling, even to laugh; everything she did was so emotional. She was more sad and angry, but at the end my mother cried because she thought her mother would stay for a long time. It'd been too painful throughout my mum's life but she held the sadness loose within her heart and there it would remain silent in her soul. Yes, her mother had gone, but the memory, a treasure to share between them both, would never leave my mum's heart.

Before, when her mother was around every morning when my mum woke up, her first thought was to find the food for her mother, and her last thought every night was to be sorry for her mother's life, but she kept all those worries inside her chest. My mum was such a beautiful daughter; she always wished she could have magic so she could make her mother's life a miracle. Anyway, my mum sat on her own, still unable to stop crying, missing her mother, who just left her in a so dark a state. Tomorrow my mum's life was going to be different, and the new life would begin, in which she would have to arrange who was going to care after the newborn, her baby sister. Straight away my mum looked at the sunset, which seemed very bright and red, like so much anger, given my mum's whole world was depressing and sad. There was so much worry in my mum's head, especially as taking responsibility of looking after her one-year-old brother was not easy, and she had to believe it but it left her blank to her life.

The next day when my mum woke up she felt her body was so tired because she'd only had one hour sleep. All night my mum couldn't stop thinking about her mother spending her first night all alone sleeping in the graveyard. And with her little brother and baby sister crying, my mum was really under pressure. But my mum comforted herself by talking to God, asking for her to be given strength for her to create her life, full of adventure.

Today was the day for my mum to arrange who was going to look after her newborn baby sister. As much as my mum loved her baby sister, she would have to give her away to someone because it was impossible for her to care for a newborn. As a twelve-year-old girl, she looked after a one-year-old boy and looked for food at the same time – more than enough for my mum. With all those problems my mum thought she would have to have a fresh new start and keep moving forward with new life in this world without her mother. Quickly my mum got up, opened all the windows, let the breeze blow, then she took a deep sip of the fresh morning air to clear her mind. The morning sun was shining and had crowned inside my mum's house. What a glorious day for my mum to begin a new chapter in her life; it seemed like a daydream for her.

My mum was a very brave young girl; she was never scared of anything. In fact she was ready to go on and continue what plan she had in her head. But my mum hoped and prayed for the better on that bright and sunny morning, that a life together with her siblings was about to begin, full of happiness. My mum was a very independent girl since a very young age; even her mother depended on her for everything, so now she knew how to find a way to live. With an empty soul, my mum sat silent, thinking that her life was like a book with many stories. Many pages with a lot of chapters, and now the beginning of another life for her. In this beautiful world nothing was perfect for nature and life, which my mum completely understood. In fact she was ready to enjoy the hustle and bustle every day in her life. A brand-new life would be very challenging for my mum, so from now on she congratulated herself from the heart and for this very new start because her journey of life would begin at any moment. Of course the sad feeling of losing of her mother would never fade away. My mum's soul would never feel free but she would have to live with it. For my mum the love and happiness she had to bring for her siblings was more important than herself, and that is how life goes. My mum keeps all the worries safely to herself, and the setting was perfect; she couldn't think of a better one. The time will lend and that is the time my mum will relief as she finally let it go. The only thing that my mom felt at that moment was all alone at home with her empty heart without her mother. My mum put herself together, but she divided her body into two, with one side of her body filled with all those memories with her mother. And those special memories with her mother made my mum's heart full of a happy smile so she could go on with her life. While the other side of her body would always cause my mum a lot of pain and sometimes she felt her body be totally numb like a dead body.

Slowly my mum took a deep breath and gently blew, then she thought, 'Well! There is so much in life and sometimes life can take a spin and be gone at the end and this is the sound of life.' Only God knows if this was a lesson to be learned for my mum. Then she looked at her little brother and wondered how she was going to explain to him about their mother, who was already gone forever. The years her little brother would have with their mother were all gone – it was too sad for my mum when she looked at her little brother. Losing her mother caused a lot of pain; it would take a little time for my mum to recover, but what she tried to do now was move on with life. Now was the time for my mum to stand on both of her feet and show to her little brother how to use his wings and learn to fly, and that is beyond the best gift.

With positive thinking in my mum's head she then picked up her little brother close to her chest, whispering to herself, saying, 'Yesterday my mother went, and yesterday everything was gone, so let's welcome today, a new chapter of life.' Also, my mum thought that yesterday had been the worst day ever in her life. But today was a little better, and she prayed that tomorrow would be better for the rest of her life.

Through the window my mum looked at the new morning sunrise as a new day brought a new light and a new beginning for her life to start fresh. Without wasting any more time my mum closed the book of her old life and began with glorious sunshine brightening her new life. This time my mum's journey would have an extra mile, but she prepared to step into it and welcome to the world full with her lives are ever ending with pressure. Also my mum prepared to step her life on a special chapter which each day passes another page, though wondered what the book would further contain.

The next day the afternoon was peaceful and calm, and the birds flew happily high to the sky. Gently my mum looked at the face of the sun with too much sadness. Anyway, my mum was outside the house waiting for the people coming to see her and her father to discuss her newborn baby sister. While my mum was waiting she then enjoyed the sunshine and played hide and seek with her little brother. That afternoon, my mum, while the sun was teasing behind the clouds, very much enjoyed spending time bonding purely with her little brother. As my mum gently stroked her little brother's hair her eyes looked deeply into her little brother's eyes and my mum felt that her little brother needed a lot of love and care. Slowly the calming breeze grew and the trees were waving free. My mum then looked at her little brother, sweat running down his body as surely as the hot sun beat down. However the afternoon changed for my mum, with her heart beating and becoming heavier, thinking of her responsibility to look after her little brother. The wind was running round their place, while my mum's eyes were blank, wide open, looking at the ground. With the afternoon sun still hanging and the leaves falling nonstop, it was like autumn had arrived; it was beautiful. Suddenly my mum thought her hands were naked at the moment but tomorrow her hands would be full of dress-up, with busy life. Slowly my mum closed her eyes, thinking tomorrow would be the day her life would make her smile, laugh, be sad and cry. But my mum couldn't wait for today's afternoon to complete the situation and surely settle like a dark cloud.

My mum rushed inside the house to look at her newborn baby sister, then whispered in her heart, saying, 'You are so beautiful, like the sun brightening the whole sky.' At any moment the people would arrive and maybe take her newborn sister away for good. So my mum took all those precious moments, spending time with her most beloved angel. In my mum's heart she wanted to spend the rest of her time looking after her newborn sister until she grew up. But that would be impossible for my mum at such a young age to look after the newborn. Anyhow, the afternoon was still young, which allowed my mum to have more special time with her newborn sister. Gently my mum snuggled and gave her newborn sister the sweetest of kisses, which made my mum forget a long, stressful day. Even though deep pains ran in my mum's heart, she reached out to hold her spirit, with her arms around her newborn sister giving all of her warmth and love.

Suddenly my mum heard someone's voice outside the house. Giving a greeting, quickly she ran to open the door. Soon my mum opened the door; she saw two women and one man who she'd never seen before. Of course, my mum already knew the reason those people were coming – obviously for her newborn baby sister. With an emotional heart my mum welcomed them and invited them inside the house. To see those people's faces made my mum's day the absolute worst day ever, even though she expecting them. But it was very sweet of my mum; she then straight away gave them a huge smile and pretended to be happy. However, those people looked very kind and nice, which put my mum's heart and mind in peace. Those people had discussed things with my mum's father – of course, she didn't know what was going on, but she hoped they would have a good talk and make the right choice. Also my mum hoped they would make their decision by listening to their heart because what they were going to have was the most precious gift. Really tough day for my mum – to think about their decision and them giving their answer was very hurtful. Especially to see her newborn sister taken away; it was the most painful thing that she was involved in in her life. There was a voice inside of my mum that whispered all day long, saying that this world could sometimes be a pretty evil and cruel place. But that is life, and sometimes it can be extraordinary good as well; nothing much we can do about it. Given my mum had no choice, she just listened to the voice that speaks inside her, which said to accept that giving away her newborn sister is the right way to do.

With all decisions done, and happy smile at those people's faces, obviously my mum's father agreed to give away her newborn sister. It didn't surprise my mum at all; she totally expected that her father would do that. Because her father would never take responsibility and had never been around to look after them. He would always spend most of his time with his second wife. With sadness in my mum's heart she prayed for her newborn sister in the safe hands of those people and that they would take good care of her for the rest of her life. Kindly my mum felt sorry for that couple because they been married for a long time but for some reason they couldn't have any children – surely her newborn sister was going to be spoiled. Even though my mum felt she'd let herself down, she knew her newborn sister would have a happy life and good future. For my mum to accept this decision was very hard for her, but she felt so proud and this was the utmost thing that she had received. Without regret my mum thought nothing was perfect in this world and life given her so many big challenges and it was difficult to accept that on her own; however she went through with it.

After they left with my mum's newborn sister, she felt the world was spinning, and it seemed sad and bleak, then tears slid slowly down her cheeks and fell to earth. My mum sat alone outside the house under the tree on the hot sunny day. Her mind wondered about so many questions and she could feel her heart break into tiny pieces at her newborn baby sister being given away. Slowly my mum took a deep breath and breathed out while praying for God to look after her newborn sister and an angel playing always around her newborn sister.

Responsibility

Last night my mum couldn't sleep all night; she was crying for hours all night thinking that after losing her mother her newborn baby sister was being taken away from her. Especially as my mum had two older sisters and older brother who stayed with another relative. My mum was only left with her one-year-old little brother and nine-year-old brother for my mum to look after. Haji Isa, my mum's father, had already left to go to his second wife, which made my mum feel like he'd ripped her heart out of her chest. With so much sadness my mum thought the only person responsible for this situation was her father, but he didn't take any action at all. He left my mum dealing with the pain and left my mum to do everything on her own. Because of her two brothers my mum chose to take responsibility, even though she was pondering her decision, but she was happy with it. And last night my mum felt so empty then she looked at her two brothers, peacefully asleep. With a smile my mum looked at her two brothers' sweet faces, which made my mum remain strong, but at the same time she was thinking how to handle this

Responsibility

pain. In the early hours my mum's whole body would start to get tired, all her energy – mentally physically and emotionally – was completely drained and would drop to the ground, but she swallowed everything then rested her pain away.

With less sleep in the morning my mum felt her head was so heavy, but she tried to put herself together because today was the day for my mum to start the most important job in her life to be done on her own. As my mum had a very strong character, she was now ready to deal with all the consequence, to learning, to face the truth and to race for her life. The most important job for her to do every day was to settle her two brothers, especially her one-year-old brother. My mum's eyes were set as an alarm clock; by 6am she'd already got, up doing the tidying and cleaning around the house before her little brother woke up. Starting from a very young age my mum has been a very clean and tidy person, so after making everything spotless she then would take her little brother to wash his body. Everything done, she would lastly feed him with the milk. And my mum's nine-year-old brother would manage to do all this by himself, which was less of a burden for my mum. But of course my mum made sure both of her brothers and herself were eating well to keep them healthy in life. How beautiful was my mum, with her relationship with her two brothers – the three of them getting on so well. Especially with her nine-year-old brother helping my mum with anything without a fight, and how amazing it is that from the start my mum did such a brilliant job. All those things came for her mother, who taught my mum how to be confident and respect each other and be kind to one another. How beautiful that my mum never threw these things away; instead she always carried and was blessed with the special gifts that she had from her mother and would have in all her life.

From the moment my mum saw her mother being taken away from this planet only two things were in her mind, like the earth and the sun. Which was that her mother left her far, far away, never to come back, unable to be touched, slowly disappearing, left with only soul and spirit coming together. But then, as soon as my mother held her little brother in her arms, straight away she knew her life would never be the same. And my mum started to feels tiredness like she'd never known it before. Of course, her daily routine would run exactly the same. And the worst nightmare was nappy-changing and the crying like a cycle, never-ending – only God would help her. Obviously, there were no afternoon naps, and two days before her mother died, that was the last time my mum had a nap. Sadly, my mum's childhood time was over, without a toy but playing on nature's lap, pure with colours, jumping in the river and climbing the trees like Tarzan. Especially dancing with the monkey, full of fun, singing and walking back home with so much happiness, full of joy without pressure. Every day for my mum was blessed, filled with great energy, without worries, and that time was extremely good without her being depressed. My mum thought she was one of the luckiest girls to have a childhood, a beautiful impression of life which is a gift, full of surprises. All those times which my mum loved and lived to the fullest and had the most enjoyable period of time, but now it was all over.

Slowly tears flowed from my mum's eyes when she thought that her childhood would never be the same and would never come back, and today everything had changed: fewer smiles, less play but more time to cry. With sadness in her heart and with no exciting childhood life, my mum hoped time would fly fast so she could see both of her brothers grow up fast. However, with her two brothers under her care my mum felt herself to be a grown-up with no time left for play, and every day she made the best of their days spent together. Unfortunately, my mum's hands were too busy throughout the day to play: washing the clothes with water, cooking, cleaning and everything. But then because of my mum's caring nature since her young age she made life great for her brothers, especially her little brother. Even though sometimes my mum's life was not exciting and becoming boring, she tried to fill those days with happiness and joy just for her little brother. Of course, my mum was struggling to forget those days of her childhood, a girl who smiled all the time. But now she cried because of the loss of her childhood that she enjoyed, like princess in the jungle. At this moment my mum just acted out her happiness to her brothers, her father and the people surrounding her, acted that her world was bright. But she was unhappy and struggled with no light of life. My mum was in the darkest room of her life and she felt that the world seemed to be unfair. But then she thought life was too shot to quarrel so she counted her blessing and asked God to protect her.

Being a twelve-year-old girl in the countryside, still considered a child, of course it was not right for my mum not to have a good childhood; it is sad. Sometimes responsibility can be hard for my mum to take, especially as she couldn't have any friends surrounding her. And there was no more freedom for my mum to do things that she liked to do, especially going to the jungle, climbing the trees and swimming free in the river. At one stage my mum got disappointed with her life, then hot words of anger came to her mind. But then when my mum looked at her little brother's face, she thought it would hurt her if she hurt the people that she cared about and loved very much. Now my mum started to notice she had a lot to learn in life and had to learn how to control herself so she wouldn't make a mistake. No one is perfect in this world, not even my mum, but she is willing to accept whatever it takes and try her very best, and that is the most important thing for her. The only time my mum got rest and had time on her own was during the night when her two brothers were asleep. That was the time she rested her mind and her body after working all day, nonstop. With a peaceful night, my mum was on her own outside the house in the dark; only light from the stars and the full moon flaring across the whole sky was watching her.

Anyhow, for my mum, her new life brought new experiences, stories to be told one day, but for now she tried to keep safe, happy and enjoy each day, week, month and year. However it really hurt my mum's heart because no one since are about her life and no one helped her. But luckily my mum knows how to survive, and of course her father did help a little – just enough to live. Sometime my mum felt a little sad because no one appreciated what she had done, not even her father, but deep down in her heart she felt so proud of herself. And my mum was so pleased that her two brothers didn't give her many problems; they both were stars. But one thing that my mum didn't like was when her little brother had a cry in the middle of the night when she was soundly asleep. While half asleep my mum felt frozen but pushed herself to get up and hoped her little brother would not have many problems. Given my mum the choice of what she has to get up for – maybe changing the nappy or wanting milk or anything. For sure that is the time to make my mum angry, upset and frustrated with the situation. But all those things my mum have to expect and accept as coming into her life. My mum genuinely enjoyed looking after her little brother though, spending time with each other, creating a close bond and growing up together; it was a blessed time for my mum. My poor mum; life was hard for her to chew sometimes, but then my mum realised this was her duty with a big responsibility.

As time went along my mum had to deal with so many things with her little brother which she'd never expected to happen. My mum had to understand that her little brother was just a year old; there would be a lot more things to come and a long way to go. But she'd thought her little brother was just a little baby, easy to take care of and play with like a toy. And now, as days and weeks passed, after not even a month she started to feel stress and pressure. All that stress and worry left my mum blank in her head;

it's so hard to explain with words, but at the same time she felt her brother gave her strength and taught her about life. So my mum promised to herself and to her late mother that as long as she was alive, whatever it took, she would look after her two brothers until the day her brothers said the words, 'I want to have my own life.'

Anyway the day was still young, plenty of time before night, while my mum was still wandering around the house with her little brother on her chest. There was still blue sky around and it was full of sunshine in every corner and for being an elder sister always have true well-wisher. My mum's life hadn't been easy, but she prayed to God for her and her two brothers to have a good life and be happy. My mum's beautiful big black eyes looked at her little brother then she thought how really blessed she was to have her little brother in her arms. Slowly my mum whispered in her heart that both of her brothers were the very best of all. And today three of them grew to find each other, sharing love with the same blood that will never fade away. From now the beats of my mum's heart were listening with little ears, saying it was really wonderful to be with her two brothers, for minutes and days, to laugh and talk, cry and smile, and pass time away, hoping happiness is around through their lifetimes. Or my mum sometimes liked to stay in the dark, where there had been no light; she then closed her eyes to block it out but inside her head they rushed about, everything. Gently my mum took a deep breath to slow it down as the oldest sister should be like a mother to her two younger brothers.

Responsibility

After only a few days my mum already started to feel that her time was getting tougher and more challenging with her little brother, and my mum also experienced waves of grief and joy. The only things my mum hoped for were that she could wash the sadness from her soul in these whispered waves and that she would be given deep strength in her life. Sometimes my mum almost gave up because there was too much of a burden on her shoulders. But her heart and soul, with her late mother's spirit whispering in her ears, said, 'Don't quit, don't quit and don't give up,' which made my mum strong right to the bone. With a smile my mum completely understood that the problem that she had is not easy to sweep away. Obviously it would take a little longer for my mum, with her two brothers, to be successful in life, but she would try her very best. Suddenly tears clouded in my mum's eyes, wondering if there were people like her or if it was just her not being able to bury her hardest times. And of course, all those hard times were not easy for my mum to carry around, but she strongly believed in herself. So, my mum strongly said, 'I am me and I am still going to stand with my two feet on the ground no matter how much hell is coming down.'

The afternoon still happy which makes my mum bring her little walking around in the jungle and pick the vegetables at the same time for their meal. After finishing picking the vegetables, my mum decided to put her little brother down on the ground and play with him. As a twelve-year-old girl my mum can be very cheeky like any other young girl. So my mum picked up a little mud and made it round and tiny, then she gave it to her little brother, pretending it was medicine. Of course, my mum didn't allow her brother to swallow it, but funnily enough her brother said, 'Yuck!'

Surprisingly, without my mum expecting it, her little brother called her with the word, 'mummy'. When my mum heard her little brother call her mummy, she was in tears inside her heart thinking of her mother giving her last breath while giving her newborn sister life. My mum started to wonder whether her little brother was going to call her mummy – just today, until tomorrow, the next week, the next month or forever. My mum looked at her little brother; he was smiling with so much joy, playing on his own. From that sweet smile my mum received, she felt love, full of life. The only wish my mum had was that one day her little brother would appreciate the times, the care, the heartache and the pain during all that times she'd cared for him. And through all her life everything my mum has been through has torn her down day by day. But my mum is a fighter; she pushes with her strength in tough times. My mum thought at this time that in the jungle she believed in herself, that life could grow and would help her to climb higher. And the blond hair my mum and her two brothers shared was an absolute miracle, especially her little brother, always super excited with everything. And they were always together, like mother and son, stuck together like glue. Today my mum gave a huge smile, with true love for her little brother, for he didn't give her too much of a problem, which made my mum very proud to call him her precious little brother. But most of the time my mum got very angry and got really tired of hearing the noisy sound of her little brother crying. It made my mum really annoyed which made her get angry at her late mother for giving birth to many children, and now she was left with her little brother for her to look after. With emotion, my mum said, 'Mum! I know since you've been gone, you've always watched over me, so I am sorry for saying these words, which I don't mean. Please forgive me, I just wish you never left the earth.'

Gently my mum took his little tiny hand with a smile but my mum looked away and hid her sadness, but stayed near the ground. My mum looked at the faraway mountains and she thought it was impossible that she could climb those mountains but without question she would have to learn how to climb. And the same thing with her situation right now: sometimes she didn't know how to handle it but without question she would have to deal with it.

Anyway, the day was getting late, but there was enough time for her and her little brother to stay in the jungle. Without wasting time my mum put her little brother on her hip and in the other hand carried vegetables. Both of them smiled to each other and my mum tried having a conversation with her little brother even though he still didn't understand but made a happy time for them both. With her hard life going on and on, it made my mum weary, worrying and lonely. But conversations with her little brother created such a beautiful soul and the strongest bonds between them both. There was time for my mum to play with her siblings; it was so great, and there were times for them to talk to each other, yet the words never came out from my mum's mouth. Because both of my mum's brothers would never understand the strain and struggle in my mum's life. Sometime my mum did try to explain to her nine-year-old brother about the situation but it got complicated and left him confused and wondering. As my mum was a person who truly cared for and loved her siblings with all her heart, she believed in herself, that she could get through it on her own with the ground that grows.

However, my mum's character could be changeable, exactly like the weather. She could be in a nightmare cloud for miles and miles travelling around. And sometimes my mum would be lost in a dark depression, not knowing how to turn back. But thanks to the power of my mum's strength she opened the window of her soul, swept up the depression and let the light shine on her future. Also my mum thanked God who gave her strength and hope for an easier way to cope in hard times. My mum had learned and been through a lot at this moment with a lot of passion. My mum realised that no one would help my mum in life and no one would get close to her; only God was closer than anyone on this planet. So every day my mum spent time on her own talking to God – it seemed her world was a blessing. And my mum was so grateful that she'd took a chance with her siblings and happy that she'd followed her heart until time would tell. But the most difficult moments of my mum's life that she tried to forget – of her late mother, the hard times and those memories – really haunted her almost every night. During the night

Responsibility

my mum always liked to be on her own looking at the stars and the full moon. But those memories haunted my mum while she had peaceful nights, asking the moon not to shine and telling the stars not to glow and telling the sky to get darker. With so much anger my mum tried to empty out of her brain, it was impossible, and she knew at this moment that her mother sat in heaven and watched every day and every thing. Anyhow, the evening started to settle and the birds started to scream, maybe calling for everyone to settle for the night while the flowers surrounding my mum's house still bloomed.

Growing Up

For my mum, growing up was very hard, especially with her two brothers. The challenges that a child must deal with throughout the life cycle are overwhelming. At a young age, she still needed to grow and to play with her friends. But instead my mum already dealt with physical, emotional and psychological things. She was without education, activity and friends but struggled with life and times, always on the next day and the following ones. However my mum never follows the fear with her fighter will always on her helping and hoping not separate from reality. My mum, such a super girl becoming a wonder woman, and from a young girl became a mother to her two brothers, may God bless her heart always. Even though her father didn't care and didn't give any support, she still continued with life – every day counting pennies to buy rice. Rice is very important for their daily basics and rice was what they were eating every day, sometimes for breakfast but for sure for lunch and dinner. Sometimes there was not much food left, just enough for one person, but my mum gave it all to her brothers and she was rather hungry going to bed. Forget about their clothes; my mum could not afford to buy things for her brothers, not even for herself. My mum's brothers only had four or five T-shirts and trousers to wear, and two pairs of slippers each, which they wore until they were torn apart. Times were hard for my mum, but she made it her life. Her brothers survived it all and grew up, becoming beautiful people. My mum always knew that she and her brothers would grow up sooner or later – it would just take a little time and she would have to be very patient. Of course my mum was very confident that she could make it through her difficult times. The overwhelming stress, frustrating and depression – my mum would fight, using the power that she had until the end. That was how my mum took responsibilities as a sister, also a mother, to care for her brothers. It was frightening for my mum sometimes to think whether they were going to be OK or not; then she thought, 'That is life and life has to go on.'

Well! Look at my mum and her brothers then: they were growing up and my mum whispered to herself, 'Let's see the peak of the earth.' There was a huge smile on my mum's face to think that she was now growing as a women and her brothers too as an adult. No more pressure and responsibility; instead my mum's brothers were worried about her life, with her going to be on her own. How funny, when my mum thought through all the years, her watching her brothers grow up strong, and now her brothers watched over my mum.

Before my mum's brothers left the house, my mum wondered what home was without her two brothers around. My mum knew soon they would be gone; the house would no longer be noisy and my mum would be on her own without a smile and the screaming would all be gone. But then my mum felt so sad that, growing up, her mother wasn't there for her little brothers. Luckily difficulties in my mum's life didn't come to destroy her two brothers. With my mum's guidance and understanding, she taught her two brothers to become good young men today. My mum followed her mother's rules by teaching them both each day every way how to behave, manners and how to respect the beauty of life. She had so much respect for her brothers and thanked them from the bottom of her heart for listening to her all the way throughout their life. Of course, there were simply not enough words to say how much they both meant to her. Especially as both of my mum's brothers were going to start their own life very soon, and that was the hardest thing: for my mum to lose them. Sadly, it was a long time ago with no phones, so without phone there was no communication between my mum and her two brothers. Very soon they were going to leave my mum, and very soon my mum couldn't hear her brothers' voice anymore, just waiting how long until they would return home. My mum's energy completely dropped when she thought about it, but she hid the pain and kept it in her heart so she wouldn't worry her brothers. My mum told her two brothers only one word which was behave. Good manners – that was what my mum taught them both. And always be honest and be true to yourself – just hold your head up and be strong; your life will be better.

Anyway, with a warm heart my mum had best wishes for her brothers for everything they did, to turn that into the best thing in their lives. In their first journey of their lives, they would have to fight challenging things and would have to be prepared. My mum prayed for her brothers' destinations. Everything starts with a new day, a new life and new things for them both to earn. And of course, for them to make it it was possible that they would have to go through tough times. My mum really hoped her brothers were prepared for this amazing adventure ride and would end up with an amazing time ahead. And my mum also hoped her brothers would take whatever opportunity and make the best out of it because the success will always be theirs. Lastly my mum hoped her brothers' lives would bring them happiness every day, the next day and for the rest. Bless my mum's heart; she had so many hopes for her brothers and became too worried.

For my mum, when her brothers moving out from her life and that is something their have to learn which is independent just like her. But sometimes without us noticing life is decided for us, but follow your dreams and make your dreams come true. My mum always gave a message to both of her brothers to remember: never forget where you come from. The time will come when both sides miss each other dearly; then my mum's brothers would have to come back to each other in a flash.

Sadly, it took my mum a while, thinking she never wanted her brothers to leave; she wished her brothers could have stayed and she did not even know how to say the words of goodbye. My mum thought she'd watched them both grow up until they'd become young men but now she couldn't afford to let them go sadly, full of tears in her heart. My poor mum; she already felt that she would forever deeply be missed, a loss for them both. Surely when her brothers left her, she would begin feeling happiness, have bad and sad times, all on her own, no more sharing with her two brothers. But with her own promise my mum was going to be strong and put a huge smile on her face just to make her brothers happy while she hid the sadness to herself.

However, my mum always reminded her brothers not to forget all the great times they'd have together and throughout their childhood the time they had shared. My mum hoped that her brothers knew how much she cared for and loved them both. And what my mum loved to hear the most was her little brothers laughing so wickedly. And that laugh make my mum stress all relieve that is a part of her brothers my going to missing. How sad my mum was to see her brothers leaving her behind, but she was not going to stop them from chasing their dream. My mum felt so wonderful and blessed to know her brothers were willing to go out and search for their new life. Both of them were so excited and so much looking forward to being independent, which they'd never experienced yet. When my mum saw the happiness on her brothers' faces she became overwhelmed then slowly my mum prayed and asked an angel in the sky to watch over them both.

Without a doubt this was the hardest thing for my mum: to let her brothers go after so many years of looking after them, but both of them would be in my mum's heart and always would be. For my mum wherever they'd go, it was only distance, she felt her brothers would always be close to her heart and not far apart. Especially as the memories would always play on her mind, never fading away, and of course she hoped her brothers did the same. My mum loved her two brothers beyond words and would miss them both beyond measure. Most of all my mum was thankful have brothers like them both, never causing any problems, just bringing words to make my mum smile on such a special day in their life, which was 'Take good care of your life and keep the same heart.'

Time flew; my mum's two brothers were no longer with her. They'd both left the house – time to find a better future. As soon as her brothers left the house, she feels completely lost like her chicks had started to fly and left the empty nest, and she wondered how she was going to find food. At that moment my mum noticed it was so tough without her brothers, after them living for so many years under her care. Hurtful tears appeared in my mum's eyes when she thought about her late mother; being a mother was surely hard for her mother sometimes. Her mother was such a wonderful woman to my mum: always understood and always smiled and was happy. Even with my mum's father her mother never once complained, just continued to look after the children and do her best and pick up all the pieces.

Anyway, my mum was left on her own without sharing the bond of care and love that my mum and her brothers had together. However, my mum thanked God for giving her two brothers to look after; because of them life had taught her everything. Especially as my mum's little brother had given her a lot of challenging times but gave her so much strength, thank goodness. With a huge smile my mum was blessed for what God had given to her and her two brothers. And amazingly her brothers never argued with her, instead always listening, which was so easy for my mum to deal with. How fantastic that my mum's brothers were always happy to play together, never fighting, biting or kicking each other. As special as can be, which helped my mum to smoothly go on with life. No words could express to her brothers that they'd made childhood for the three of them the best, with happy memories to be remembered for the rest of her life. Then my mum thought there was no love like the love of our own blood, and they owed so much happiness to each other. And my mum would rather not have friends because she thought her brothers were worth a thousand of her friends – how beautiful my mum's heart is.

However, my mum always reminded her brothers that the key of happiness was to come forward and talk to her – whatever problem they had, my mum was always there to listen. For my mum, her two brothers were like diamonds sparkling, flashing forever in her heart. Not just brothers but her friends too; as life went along my mum and her brothers learnt every mistake they each had made and taught one another lifelong lessons.

When her late mother was still alive she always talked to my mum about so many things in life. My mum received some very good advice from her late mother which my mum would always program in her brain. And one particular

Growing Up

piece of advice her mother had told her was that the blood that flows through my mum's veins is the same blood that flows in my mum brothers' veins. So now my mum understood what the meaning of that sentence was that her late mother had said. With eyes closed, my mum thought her late mother was absolutely right – yes, the same blood would always be in our life. My mum and her brothers had grown up together and now life was making them moving apart. My mum's brothers were like her sons; surely the distance would make the three of them stronger, but their hearts moved faster every time, thinking about each other. Of course, my mum knew that being brothers and sister meant being there for each other, and how fantastic it was that they'd been with each other since a young age. Once my mum's brothers left, she then straight away held on to their memories and company for her to continue with life. Since my mum's brothers had grown up, she could count on them always. Especially as my mum had become beautiful; young ladies always need them around for protection.

Anyway, my mum was so proud of her brothers; both of them really cared for and stood up for my mum if anything happened. All my mum's time, energy, pressure and struggling to look after her brothers was paying off with so much satisfaction. A day they're together this is what my mum earns about the bond of sister and brothers and their relationship truly priceless which hardly anyone can have it. Simply my mum said to herself, in a world where you can be anything, be nothing but yourself. For her brothers from the secrets of her pinkie promise they would always be a part of my mum's world.

Anyway, for a long time my mum's two brothers gave her a very busy life through all the years until she never knew the meaning of being lonely and relaxed. And my mum also never knew that her life could feel so different until they were both gone. The only thing that my mum did know was that she was missing her brothers dearly and now she understood what the meaning of loneliness was. The loneliness made my mum feeling completely lost, scared and worried without her brothers around, which she never felt like before. Well, my mum should be happy because she had more time for herself to do everything what she wanted to do. But not for my mum; she can't sit around doing nothing. She felt everything seemed down because she was not used to this kind of life. Honestly, since my mum's brothers had gone and left her behind, she felt nothing around her was beautiful since her world had gone silent and mute. During the day my mum always sat outside the house on her own looking at a lonely cloud silently without a sign, exactly like her at the moment.

On one particular afternoon while my mum watched the sun come up and begin to rise she thought that life would have to go on without her brothers. Of course, things were not going to be the same when she was without her brothers, and surely my mum was going to be sad, with the love within her heart and silent tears without her brothers. It was really hard for my mum to get through one day without her brothers; she felt weak and helpless not watching over them each day. Especially during the night; my mum always watched over her brothers as they fell asleep. And my mum gently touched her little brother's head, slowly stroking then whispering, 'Be a good boy.' But now she was all alone in the darkness with her tears. Slowly my mum closed her eyes and remembered all the memories with her brothers, especially her little brother's laugh, making her smile. Most of the time my mum couldn't really sleep during the night, thinking tomorrow would start, a day without her brothers. She felt like she had been alone for a lifetime.

All this time my mum's life had been busy, caring for her brothers, until she didn't have time for herself. So now my mum took her precious time, sitting and thinking about the years that had passed by. The beautiful memories of her late mother; without noticing, my mum's tears had once again begun. It just showed how much she was missing her late mother. And the happiness and joy, memories of life with her brothers, hard times, bad times, all of those bringing a smile and all the fun. My mum didn't even know it until this time, which made her laugh when she thought about it, but now life had never been the same again without them.

My mum remembered her mother gave her and siblings loads of love, everything that she could give, and there was nothing they couldn't beat. Luckily for my mum, before her mother died, she taught my mum how to fight and how to never give up in life. And the last beautiful words her mother told my mum that always sang in her ears which she would never forget. Her mother also told her, 'Remember, always look after your future because new days will come and tomorrow is another day to live.' And lastly her mother said, 'The clouds and the skies are together but will never mix with the rain. And the same with our heavy heart and tears in our eyes: they stay in the same body but will never mix together.' So, with all those memories my mum slowly looked up to the sky with her message to her late mother, saying that two of her sons were growing up into beautiful young men. Surely that was what her mother was missing. A huge smile grew on my mum's face with another message to her late mother says that she brought her love during my mum thirst and she keep that love last uttered. My mum hoped her late mother looked down on her and appreciated all the good things that she'd done for her brothers with warm heart and hands that really helped in life.

But from then on my mum strongly made her promise to hide her heartache and accepted living her life without her brothers and to live on beyond the veil. My mum also promise she would comfort herself from the sadness and pain, hoping for the best. From then my mum was not going to say the words 'feeling sad' – that would be a bit too shallow, but words just couldn't explain how she was feeling. My mum was feeling so low with her mother's life taken away, and now her brothers had left her to search for their new future, which my mum completely understood.

For the first weeks without her brothers my mum was lonely during the day and lonely during the night, and she was lonely in so many ways. Especially in the house where my mum grew up with her brothers; it was the most loneliest place which brought her tears almost every day. Amazingly my mum's loneliness made her life so calm, bringing back her childhood time enjoying things with nature. As a promise my mum wouldn't allowed the sorrow and the darkness to wrap her up; instead of that, she enjoyed many kinds of birds singing in the jungle and flying over her. To hear the sound of bamboo crashing by the winds while a cloud withdrew from the sky was absolutely glorious, and the world was rather great. My mum's favourite thing to do was something truly magical, which was her secret to a good morning: to stand in front of the mountain to see the sun climbing up the mountain. As soon as the sunrise climbed the mountain, with an open heart the first thing my mum did was a tiny dance full of happiness. My mum opened her big eyes when she saw magnificent colours – amber and red and orange – catching the trees and awaking the sky; it was a breathtaking beauty. A new day began and for another day my mum prayed from her heart for her life to make her smile. And to see the sun with a beautiful smile to brighten the world just made my mum's day fresh for her to start a new chapter of her life.

Sometimes in the afternoon my mum would come back to see the sun reach the peak of the mountain. But most of the time my mum stayed in the house because the weather was too hot and humid. From the window my mum watched the afternoon sun hanging high in the sky with so much joy.

And my mum would finally return to end the day and to see the sun fall to the river and bring the beautiful colour of the sunset. My mum would stand silently, focused on the beauty of the soft orange and slowly waving goodnight. Then, seeing the birds returning to their nests, my mum would gently say goodbye to the sunset, although she hated to see the sun go. It was amazing, but suddenly everything continued to change and within a minute the world grew dark, surrounding my mum. My mum was in love with the sunset, but it was a joyful privilege to enjoy all day with the sun, and tomorrow was another day when she would wait for the sun to rise.

From this moment my mum started to enjoy herself, being in her own company, and she loved spending time with herself. Funnily enough my mum actually started to be so happy, being able to do what she felt like, which she had never had for a long time after her mother died. So now what my mum wanted was to turn that last page of a book – to have someone in her life.

Married Life

One hot afternoon my mum looked through the window and the sun had risen, smiling at her, and she thought, 'What a marvellous day.' The weather was so hot and sticky, and sweat ran down my mum's body so she decided to go to the river to cool down. By foot, my mum walked alone to the jungle while the rubber trees swung around, blown by the winds. After more or less fifteen minutes my mum had arrived and was sitting by the river. There was nothing much in my mum's mind except thoughts about her life, and of course another day to be on her own. My mum looked into the river and the wind blew down, creating ripples flowing in the water; it was superb. With the glistening sun, blue sky, the greenest surroundings and the fragrance of wildflowers, that was enough for my mum to cheer her day. And to see the river flowing down its path with all that beauty of nature, my mum realised the world is a magical place which made her heart so peaceful. My mum's face was full of a smile but she still sat by the river on the edge of the waterfall, marvellous happiness buried inside her.

But from that moment my mum thought, where should she start her new life, and with who, when suddenly someone's footsteps interrupted her thoughts. As soon as my mum looked she saw it was a man standing in front of her, which made my mum's heart skipped a beat. With shock and without any words and without a blink my mum just looked at him. But my mum had so much worry and was scared thinking about what was going to happened to her. Suddenly that guy gave a glorious smile to my mum, which made my mum trust him, but in my mum's head she wondered who man this man was, who she'd never seen before. There was a whisper in my mum's heart with the words, wow! To see that smile, it was so pure and true, made my mum speechless for the first time in her life. However my mum was ready for everything; if he came closer she knew what to do, especially as my mum was a very brave woman. In secret my mum's eyes fluttered, seeing how tall he was and how fair his skin was. His face all seemed so perfect; my mum spoke words only in her heart: that he was her ideal man.

My mum had never experienced this kind of feeling before and she'd never had this kind of feeling until she laid eyes on him. But then straight away she questioned herself: is there such a thing as love at first sight? Again she questioned herself: how is it possible to feel so much for a stranger – ummm… so weird. But then my mum thought it could be love; love can be blind and love has no limit. That was when she realised she had fallen in love at first sight.

With his kindness he offered to help my mum to get up, and with no excuse she straight away accepted the offer.

With his hand in my mum's hand and with a touch like electricity straight to her body, the feeling was sensational. Only God knew how my mum felt, which no one would understand, but my mum played it cool and kept it as a deep dark secret. And with those feelings my mum's heart whispered, 'That's the one, he is the only one for me,' and gave all of herself to him. Since that first time they'd meet without a plan, and since that time the relationship continued with them meeting each other by the river; and the river was their dating place.

That was the first time my mum fell in love, and life didn't make things that easy for my mum, but when he told my mum that he was in love with her, it was a magical moment for my mum. Aww! My mum's heart almost dropped to the ground; she was over the moon, wanted to scream to the whole world that her life had brought a light of happiness; it felt so marvellous. And that is what is called true love: when the two hearts met straight away my mum knew that love had finally found her. Even though my mum had feelings for him, she kept the secret in the darkness, but now her panic was arising and my mum was ready, for the first time out of words, to say, 'I am in love with you too, and yes, I truly love you.'

Since both of them had expressed their feelings to each other, from that time every day my mum couldn't stop thinking of him. First thing when my mum opened her eyes in the morning her mind was all over him. And every night she slept with a huge smile on her face; at this moment her life was very special. Day after day after day, they hold each other's heart with care and loving, which made them love each other forever. Love is amazing, changed my mum's life completely, especially as she started dressing herself well and she always looked with a glowing face and good communication with people.

Suddenly my mum's life had changed; like the sun she felt her heart from a distance. Because she had to leave her lover with so much pain, knowing her father had an arrange marriage planned with someone else. With so much heartbreak my mum stood in the dark crying and truly she felt a loss of the love of her life. But my mum had stolen his heart and that would with her forever; that is how cruel love can be.

For my mum to marry someone who she was not in love with was not easy: getting to start a life and to force a relationship to grow. My mum would never be forced to love him, especially as their hearts and minds never met and with both of them totally coming from a different world. He appeared in front of my mum's house – a handsome tall man with fair skin – but my mum couldn't care less. And my mum didn't care to dress herself up; in fact she just wore a sarong and a big flabby cotton T-shirt. My mum just stayed inside the house, not even offering to come in, and no words were exchanged. Because my mum's father was together with them, of course as a very traditional introduction, my mum had to serve him a tea. With so much anger in my mum's heart to her hater for arranged to marriages without discuss with her nothing. When they left my mum did not even say goodbye and did not even see her future husband's face. How my mum support to see his face when she felt utter stranger especially no feeling what so ever. My mum knew a marriage with him would be a marriage from hell; she would rather be all by herself than marry that man. But there was nothing much my mum could do about it because it was her father's decision and he purely acted for his wealth. Sadly, my mum's father never thought about her happiness and he just thought about the money. What most frightened my mum was that he was younger than my mum; for sure he'd never thought about life. Instead he was wild and free. At that moment my mum felt like a little bird trapped in a cage and she wanted to fly high to the sky then disappear in the mountain clouds. My mum felt so sick about her father because due to his wealth he would make her trapped forever. Because my mum knew her father never loved her; that was why he didn't care whether a man was right or wrong for her. This unique relationship followed the generations for a very long time but was less certain when it came to my mum's generation. However, my mum still respected her father's decision with this old custom, which would win forever.

The time had come for my mum to celebrate the best day of a girl's life, but of course not for my mum; it was the worst and saddest day of her life. Especially as she had to leave her lover and marry a stranger. Today was my mum's wedding day; she was eighteen years old and forced to marry a young sixteen-year-old boy. And she was forced into a situation that my mum didn't choose, which made my mum so emotional, bringing floods of tears to her heart. Since a young age my mum had always wanted her life to be happy, but right now she had to pretend in front of her father with others that her marriage was amazing. To face herself and pretend was truly a horrible thing to do in the world. Luckily the wedding was simple; it was just getting my mum and that man to start a life, but she couldn't force herself to love him just because he was her husband.

The wedding was all over and my mum thought that arranged marriages are such a funny concept, like a toy. It reminded her of when she was a young girl playing at marriages with friends. Whatever it was, my mum would have to prepare for the next day to start her new life. But my mum was so happy to find out after the wedding that the husband, despairing, did not come back home for the rest of the night. The happiest thing ever for my mum, not to sleep with a stranger, and she hoped the marriage would not last forever. After a week her mother-in-law came to see my mum and told my mum that her son was staying with her and her mother-in-law suggested for my mum to get him. My mum looked at her mother-in-law without a word; she thought, 'No way am I going to get your son back home, and thank God for his cleverness.' He was a young boy and looked attractive but was not smart enough for my mum.

Funny enough, after he returned home to his bride without explaining, admitting guilt or anything, he just played damn stupid. My mum's life with him start to get stressful because he was a very lazy man; he liked to sleep, didn't like to work and didn't know how to take responsibility as a husband. It gave my mum no choice; she would have to work hard to bring food to the table.

If my mum said something straight away he'd get angry, aggressive; it ended the argument then he would hit my mum. My poor mum – so many bruises around her body, but my mum still continued life with him with a broken heart. So they didn't have good conversations between them, just living under the same roof but as different people. After a few days one morning, shockingly to my mum, without expecting she found out she was pregnant. Sadly my mum was so worried and she wondered how she'd got pregnant quicker than she expected. As soon as my mum told her husband about her pregnancy he got mad and accused my mum of having a relationship with another man. The pregnancy made their marriage worse and day after day my mum stayed under pressure, but she bore with him to save the marriage.

One afternoon my mum waited for her husband to return home; at the same time her eyes looked at the old clock on the wall moving, showing it was almost late evening. Of course my mum was worried but she was more worried about herself all alone. So my mum started to lock the door and clear away the dinner that she'd prepared for her husband. The next day my mum's husband still did not come back, which continued for the rest of the day, then for weeks and months. which made my mum feels so down, especially as he left the house without a single word. What kind of man he was: no sympathy for a pregnant woman left all alone by herself. He was such an idiot with an evil heart.

Anyway, the time had almost arrived for my mum to give birth; she of course was very scared and worried on her own. She didn't know what to do, especially for her first child. So, my mum packed a few clothes in the plastic bag then she decided to give birth in her uncle's house. My mum's uncle's house was the place that she could ask for help, even though she knew her uncle's new wife was a very nasty woman but she had no choice. Soon my mum arrived at her uncle's house; he was very happy to see my mum, especially for her to give birth at his house. But not my mum's uncle's horrible wife; when my mum looked at her, her face turned evil, which my mum expected from her. Luckily, my mum didn't wait for long to give birth to a beautiful baby girl, which was me being welcomed to the world. My mum's uncle was so happy and adored me so much; he even gave me my name, Azizah, which made his wife so jealous. But my mum's uncle couldn't care less about his wife, just continuing to do what he was doing. Of course my mum was the person who received bad treatment from her uncle's wife day after day after weeks until my mum had enough and decided to go back to her house. My mum's uncle was very sad because he loved Azizah so much, but on the other hand he understood about his wife's behaviour, like a witch. The next day my mum carried a few plastic bags with her clothes and the newborn baby girl inside.

At last my mum happily settled at her own home, but sadly with the baby still tiny, she couldn't go out for work and to get the food for her and her baby. With her hunger and with her shamelessness, she forced herself to ask for a bowl of rice from her neighbour. And sometimes my mum slept with an empty stomach; luckily the baby had her breast-feeding. But most of the time my mum searched the house's surroundings for whatever vegetables or potatoes that she could make a meal for her and the baby out of. The meals for a day settled, tomorrow was another day; that was how my mum continued her everyday life. Difficulties had just been a part of my mum's life since a young age, with happiness coming after difficulties. But then all of a sudden everything stopped and huge pain took over her. For example, my mum was happy in life when her late mother was around, but then she hurt badly when suddenly her mother left her forever. Then my mum was so happy to look after her two brothers even though life was very tough for her, but then she got hurt the day her brothers left her all alone. Again, my mum was a very happy woman in the world when she found love with the love of her life, but she got hurt again when she had to leave him and marry someone else. I'm so proud of my mum; she was still strong and could continue with her life. In fact she said, 'Life can be the sunshine on a beautiful day but can change the next minute with clouds, and suddenly pour with raindrops, exactly like how human happiness can turn to sadness and burst into tears.' This made my mum question herself when every single thing happened but she never got the answer. Well, my mum was a tough woman; whatever happened in her life, she continued to live with it and made her way through each raw minute. Life was hard for my mum; however she felt so blessed and very grateful in this moment to have a roof over her head. My mum was a survivor; she survived a lot of things in her life and she had such a strong heart even though she struggled so much. But my mum wouldn't give up and she never waited for something to fall from the sky, just like her late mother.

Anyway, from then my mum felt her life was so much better without her husband, but she was still waiting and hoping for him to come back home because they were still husband and wife.

Surprisingly, after long six months' waiting, finally my mum's husband returned home. My mum looked at his face and she thought, 'Wow, he's still alive and he knows how to come home.' Not many words were exchanged between them and my mum just went with the flow but of course she accepted him. I feel so sorry for my mum because she knew her husband was so absurd but deep in my mum's heart she needed someone in her life, especially with the baby. And my mum thought that maybe her husband was young; she just hoped it wouldn't happen again.

The happiness lasted only a few weeks sadly; after a small issue my mum's husband made big problem and started an argument between them both. Especially with my mum's husband being very aggressive, full of a temper, it ended with my mum get kicks and slaps from him. My poor mum; she bore all that pain. Only tears comforted her bleeding heart. No family, no relatives and no friends to help my mum with her husband's behaviour towards her. Also he was a very lazy man: didn't want to go to work, to take responsibility as a husband, only depending on my mum. My mum had to wake up in the early hours to do the rubber tippers and come home, prepare food for him, do everything for him – what a life he had. But then again, my mum was pregnant with a second child, and again he left my mum without any word; after a week my mum give birth. He repeated the same thing he did for his first baby, the second, the third and the fourth, but it was not as bad as with the first one. Bless my mum's heart; she had to keep up with her husband's behaviour. What he did was like a game for him – surely he had fun.

All that mess in her life made my mum start to think about her first lover, so beautiful a person. She thought her life would have so much happiness if she was with him. Without noticing tears started falling down her face; honestly my mum really missed him and she always missed him. So much heartbreak; my mum cried for hours, angry with her father, marrying her to a man who was a boy. Through their marriage my mum couldn't feel any love at all; as time went on that boy just ran forward and backward like a yoyo, and she just watched until their marriage failed. From the beginning of their marriage he never put any effort into their relationship, which left my mum with a fake smile and fake everything.

Of course, my mum felt sad to run away from her husband, but my mum didn't feel guilty about her decision. He would never change his bad behaviour, even though he kept promising a million times to not do it again; they were just words. And a million times he broke his promises, which left my mum really heartbroken; they seemed to never go away. One thing that my mum knew: once a cheater always a cheater, and her husband cheated when the first baby was born then continued until the fourth child and he would never stop. So leaving him behind was all my mum could do to make her life much easier to live. For my mum, even though her husband didn't spend much time with her, the time that they'd had was suffering enough and eating her inside badly. That suffering made my mum become so strong, strong enough that she could walk away, leave that boy behind so he would grow and learn everything in life.

With my mum's anger running like a fire, without wasting any more time, her mind got really mad, all about her husband, thinking about what he done to her life. With my mum's heart burning like flames out of control, the time was coming that she couldn't tolerate any time with him any longer. With so much anger she became so brave, packing all of her and all her four children's things, but left her house and everything behind, including her husband.

With some help the next day my mum was in different town with her children starting a fresh new life without her husband. After three days my mum got a new place where she finally could breathe and smile a little smile after a long, miserable life with him. One evening really shocked my mum's whole system and she couldn't believe her eyes, what he done and he still needed her when it was over. But for my mum, as soon she saw her husband face the fire burning inside her body like a volcano, there was no turning back, and for her, her feeling towards him were completely like an empty shell.

Again a few more things happened that my mum would still have to deal with, until her stupid husband finally ended things with divorce – I was thankful that my mum's life was safe at last. From all those experiences my mum learnt every day from the mistake she had made, and she became an even stronger person to deal with the pain. With a strong heart my mum thought to never give up on life so she would use the pain as fuel to make her future better. As my mum is a very clever woman she knew no one life would ever be perfect, so that's why she didn't sit around waiting for something to come, and for her it wouldn't work that way. So, with her brain she could choose to believe in the light even when she was stuck in the darkness.

Anyhow, my mum thought that is life; every new beginning sometimes comes from some an end. But every time my mum got hit by her husband made her alive again. Every time he ran away from the responsibility was another time my mum closed her heart with a different word spoken. And every time he returned home my mum never looked at his face because his eyes told a lie story. Most of the time my mum sat on her own crying in the dark, full of anger and pain. Before my mum ended her marriage with her husband, she never thought twice; instead she could feel that the time had come for her to leave him and for her to be free. To see his awful behaviour, to hold the pain of his temper and to stop tears with so much sadness, my mum thought she'd rather be alone than hide behind the blindfold. This time, whatever words he told my mum, she would never trust him again, especially as he was too lazy to work and treated her like a slave. Every time when my mum's husband despaired she was tears, full of blood, every morning, day and night, agony falling from her broken heart. My mum tried so hard to save their marriage and for not a single moment did she think they would part ways. But now that she gone forever in his life has become not return back.

Anyway, my mum had now left peacefully with her four children, without a stressful life, only knowing that the world and the people out there are complicated. The getting less makes very difference when the tears not running down on the cheeks. Sometimes my mum was very scared to be alone with four children without a husband: another big responsibility which reminded her of when she looked after her two brothers. Sadly my mum's life never give her peace and happiness, and she never ran away from the problem. Suddenly out of the blue her husband came to find her.

The broken marriage made my mum become even stronger and a more positive person, fighting for the negatives to stay out of the fire to save her life. However, my mum thanked God for saving her life and thanked God that her marriage would not take a lifetime. For many years my mum suffered in silence and was hurt badly, not able to recover while spending every night in tears in the darkness. My mum was left all alone with a broken heart with not a word that could be spoken.

A New Life Begins

In this world there was nothing more that my mum could think of but building her new life with her four children. And her children's lives were the mean reason making my mum think about where and how to begin planning for their future. In my mum's heart she loved to live in beautiful life with her children, but it had not been easy for my mum, especially as life was far from perfect. My mum totally understood where she was coming from but the circumstances in her life made her very frustrated, especially for her children. Thank God, since my mum had left her husband she'd done a marvellous job for her life, with a happy and smiling face without any pressure, even though financially there was a bit of a problem at this stage.

My mother didn't have a lot of education, but she is very smart in the head and courageous in the heart, confident herself, and compassionate in her thoughts.

As time went on the tasks eternally grew; life moved forward; all the sadness in her heart brought flowing tears to her eyes. One good thing about my mum is that she always remembers three things in her life, which are: God is with her, still with her and always with her. And time for my mum was so precious and time never waited for anybody; it just ran like water. In life my mum never waited for time; she always had something to do and she always chased the time. But sometimes it did happen when time would pass; my mum got really frustrated because she knew the time that she would never want to repeat again. So, my mum thought she would enjoy every moment in her life with her four beautiful children. If any bad things happened in her life, as she always had, she never compared herself with others. And my mum would never close the book; instead she just turned the page and began a new chapter of her life. For my mum she believed every person's life was like a book because every new day of a life was a new chapter of life. My mum was a very clever woman. That was my mum's life, exactly like a book; some chapters are interesting and some are exciting but most are sad. But from now on my mum didn't want to turn the page because she didn't want to know what the next chapter held.

With every mistake that my mum made in her life she learnt from those experiences. And with my mum, she was a strong believer that whatever mistake she made, it was never too late for her to become who she wanted to be. For the journey of life my mum had fought for many years about so many things especially her focus to live a life that her children could be proud of, and I am so proud that she was my mother.

My mum loved to sing; in fact, she had such a beautiful sweet voice and she loved to play traditional Malay music, but of course not a piano. Well, at that time there were no pianos and she didn't not even know what a piano is. However, my mum loved to play one particular traditional Malay game called congkak and she played almost every day. Congkak has to be played with two players, but my mum always played on her own. The reason my mum loved to play congkak was because she thought her life was exactly like congkak. And congkak uses almost a hundred marbles with so many different kinds of colours; also congkak consists of fourteen small holes and all those holes will be filled up with marble. As soon as my mum started to play and touched all those marbles, the sound of it were happy days for my mum. But then when my mum lost the game, she got a little upset but somehow made her think that was the part of the game. Or my mum needed another player to make the game fun or challenging. The same thing with life; my mum thought life sometimes can be very complicated, but never ran from the problems, it always being stressful. But from the beginning of my mum's life she always counted her blessings especially now in her life she learnt how to be happy.

Suddenly the silence of midnight was broken by the sound of raindrops falling from the heavens, hitting against the roof. My mum took a slow walk to the room to check her four children were well, everyone cuddled up warmly and soundly asleep. My mum left them all asleep and enjoying their dreams while walking back to sit in the living room. For some reason it was so hard for my mum to sleep that night. The night was silent but there was the sound of a mosquito flying around my mum, trying to get her blood, but my mum's hand within a second killed that mosquito. And the night insects and the frogs screaming outside, surely enjoying playing in the rain. Suddenly, bang – the sound of loud thunder – and that was loud enough to wake all the memories inside her. The life of raindrops and the sound of thunder haunted my mum's brain, which brought tears to her eyes, but she tried to hold it, not to drop it. To keep my mum's emotions strong, not to drop to the ground, through the window she tried to see any stars to wish on or the full moon, but there were none: it was completely dark. But instead, my mum listened to more rain beating, creating melodies and symphonies of life which brought a smile on my mum's face. Anyway, my mum realised with her sadness that nature can bring the joy of life without a plan – what splendid midnight rain for my mum.

Last night my mum didn't sleep much but she still woke up early with a huge smile on her face, a fresh beginning to start her new life. Quickly my mum opened the window to see the weather outside and with her gentle voice she said, 'Oh wow, it's going to be a great day today.' It was just 6.30am but the feeling of humidity started running all over my mum body, but her mind focused, knowing that she was going to enjoy hustle and bustle of the day. With a smile my mum thought that life is a gift and so far God had always been kind to her and always given her another life to live. Without a doubt life was full of challenges; as always my mum accepted the challenge as a journey to be enjoyed. It was tough for my mum, life as a single mother with four children. But not for a single second did she regret the decision she had to make because she believed life made the decision for her. And once my mum took her footsteps, she would never look back; instead she kept moving forward, and this was her character: a very proud and strong woman. On this humid morning my mum's heart jumped around, full of energy for a brand-new day and yesterday was gone. My mum whispered to herself, 'Yes, yesterday was not bad, today is wonderful and I hope tomorrow and forever will be perfect life without any pressure.'

Anyhow, my mum couldn't wait to start work as a rubber tapper, but with the rainy season my mum had no choice but to wait until the rainy season was over. My mum started to get worried, and waiting for rain to stop is the hardest thing, especially with no income incoming for their daily basics. The only thing my mum could do at that moment was just watch the leaves all falling to the ground. Which made my mum think of all those leaves, wishing they were money falling to the ground which made her life so much easier.

After more than a week's rain nonstop suddenly, today the sky had good news for my mum. The rainy season finally over, it was time for my mum to start a life that would be full of joy and always bring the happiness that she was waiting for. Many women embarrass themselves doing the rubber tapper because it's very dirty and smelly; of course, only poor people do this kind of job. For my mum, she couldn't wait; this was how my mum lived her life, and she enjoyed tapping every single rubber tree that she tapped. Even though the money was just enough to pay the rent and food, at least she didn't beg people for the money. My mum lived simply but she was so very grateful at this stage to have a roof to put over her children's head and food on the table. And the most important was my mum's health; especially during the night she slept soundly and this was the secret of her happiness. In fact, she taught all of her four children to be happy with what they had and to appreciate every single thing in their life. At this time of my mum's life, she would try not to touch the same water twice because the water flow that passed would never pass again. My mum thought that before she would cry because she had no food, but now she would smile because she had more than enough food to feed her children.

My mum never got tired; I just wonder how she found the energy to do everything – just imagine she was a husband, she was a wife and she was a mother. Most of the time my mum's life was filled with hard times rather than good times, but she never moaned – such an amazing woman. Even though my mum's times were always hard, she kept the pain inside her and felt the pain on her own without sharing it with anyone. When myself and my three brothers were kids my mum gave us the world, put it right at our feet and taught us to never lose sight. I am thankful for my mum, who taught me to become who I am today. Even though the hard times of my mum's life were so tough, she still tried her very best, giving her children everything they needed.

To support her four children, especially with every single one of us going to school, of course my mum need to prepare more money. To pay for the rent, the bills and the food my mum had to work around the clock; from 4am she was already out to do the rubber tapper. After finishing doing the rubber tapper my mum did not even have a rest; she rushed to go to the restaurant to work as a helper chopping the vegetables, cleaning the floor and washing the plates. My mum was very tired but she was happy at the same time because working at the restaurant the owner allowed her to bring back whatever food was leftover. With all that food my mum could save some money for other things and sometimes I made that food last for a couple of days. As far as I remember my mum worked hard for every one of us; she did not even have time for herself. The only time my mum had was when she slept; I can't even imagine the sacrifice it took for my mum to be a wife, husband and a mother – wow, she is one in a million, an absolutely amazing woman. With her work around the clock, my mum still smiled and her smile was more beautiful than flowers opening in the morning.

My relationship with my mum was very funny; we never got along for long as we both always had a problem, because we both have very strong characters with strong opinions. Even though my mum and myself argued a lot, whatever happened my mum would always be there for me and at the end of the day she was my mother, my best friend in all the world since I was young. We talked about a lot of things, but the most special and precious moment was when she talked about her childhood, growing up without a mother at a very young age. In fact my mum told me everything in detail about her life, which brought me to tears to hear the story of my mum at the age of twelve years old. And with her being a hard-working woman she was the most wonderful mother, a treasure that can never be replaced. But one thing about my mum's character was that she was a very tough cookie; she wouldn't listen to anyone and she always had her own opinion.

Anyway, my mum was very openminded; as we are Muslims, of course we respect and are very proud of our religion. But my mum was one of those people who like to live life in freedom and who don't like to force their children to follow the rule of Islam. What I love about my mum is that she always helped people and she had such a beautiful heart which was made of gold, and without her in my life I wouldn't know what to do. Not just her heart is beautiful; she has a beautiful face too and I am so proud of my mum, knowing that she always cared about her beauty, especially when she did her make-up – it never went wrong. The colour of her make-up must fit with the colour of her dress just like the celebrities. My mum showed me her beauty and her caring about her beauty, which made me follow in her footsteps. Seeing that this was my mum, I prayed to God every day to give her great happiness in her life, full of deep blessings. Amazingly my mum years with all her tears for many thousand things she has done for so many years, she gives her life for us and to be my lifelong friend because you are brilliant and precious mother.

Honestly, I never knew a wonder woman like my mum; she was strong, she was a fighter, never letting herself down and never giving up in life. She was the most enlightened and was more committed than a mother. Sadly my mum never showed her love towards us, especially with her busy life; she just thought about her tiredness and money, but I'm sure she held her children in her heart forever.

I've always been very proud of my mum because she was one of the amazing women called a mother and she was one of beautiful women that I've ever known. My mum's two stunning cheekbones made people fall in love as soon as she smiled and it was hard to forget, simply ravishing. My mum really cared about her beauty; for her beauty was part of her life, which made her happy, especially when people said, 'You are beautiful.' So funny – my mum wouldn't go out without her make-up, lipstick especially was very important for her – and I am exactly like her.

I would do everything to make her happy because she had a hard time when she was with her husband and she worked hard in her life since her divorce. And of course I have only one mother in the wide world and there is nothing on earth more beautiful to me than my mum's smile, especially her wicked laughter which just makes me happy. My mum's glowing brown eyes were the warmest colour, like a magic moment, which made her life more beautiful and everyone thought her life was so perfect. And her oily dark-toned skin; it was so perfect a bloom, so pure from God's creation, and this was my mother.

My mum's responsibility to look after her four children was with every one of us who she trained to become a good person. So now was the time for us to take responsibility for our future; every one of us got a job, some with their own business and myself with my career. I am a little different compare with others; I like a beautiful life and like to be glamorous. My life is my decision and no one can tell me who I am; this is exactly like my mum's character. Now was the time for my mum to rest herself for the hard work she'd done all her life, especially to inspire me to see the world. My mum, like a fortune-teller, could tell every one of our futures. And for myself she said I would go far away to a different country because I have a mole under my feet – so funny but she was absolutely right. Anyhow, when my mum said those words I was so excited, full of a smile, because I love travelling and I love adventure, knowing new things in life.

I sit on my own, thinking about responsibility, meaning that I could do everything on my own and I could be free and responsible. Even though I could be free, my mum was a women with a straight rule and I will always be sticking to her rules. I still ponder my decision, especially thinking about my mum; she never had a perfect childhood and never had a perfect life; neither do her children. I couldn't wait to hold a key to my life to search for a better future and to give my mum a marvellous life that she'd never had before. I believe to have something that you dream for, you must fight, so I will fight until the end, especially for my mum.

At last, my mum gave me the key to my heart, including the wings – wow, now I can fly high like a bird looking down at the ground, an absolutely glorious time. Sadly, my mum was not very happy to let me go and sadly she didn't know where I was flying to. But I had confidence and trust in myself with this decision that I made for my mum's future. From then my focus was to make my life a success and to give the best for my mum's life and to make her proud. I never promised my mum but I promised my heart that I would look after her until the day she died. Every day in my life, first thing in the morning when I opened my eyes, I was think about how to make her happy. My heart whispered, 'Please, God, look after my mum until I achieve my dream – I love her today and I love her forever.'

The time was flying by, again with my mum on her own; it reminded her of when her brothers left her. But she was a very strong woman and took it peacefully and calmly. Surely for a few days, weeks and months my mum's heart was filled with memories of her children. My mum and myself had a sad childhood and were always torn from my cruel father, but we both survived it all. I was now growing up as a strong independent woman, but those bad memories are something I will never forget.

One evening my mum was sitting on her own on the swing outside the house when suddenly silent tears came to her eyes, thinking that all her children had gone to have their own life. Of course, my mum understood, but she never expected for time to go so fast and she had not prepared to ever say goodbye to all her children. Tears were still running down my mum's cheek but at the same time she smiled when she looked back on all those memories of her children – they were just a treasure for her. Slowly my mum closed her eyes and, with her heart, whispered, 'Please, God, keep their lives safe always and hold them with your care until they are reunited with me.'

After a few months my mum started to settle herself and she started to feel her life was completely new for the first time in her life without responsibility, just needing to look after herself. As time went along my mum didn't feel alone anymore; she started to have a lot of friends and enjoy those special times in her life. In my mum's free time she loved picking roses – almost every house got roses. Most of the roses were red and pink, but my mum's favourite rose was the white rose – the smell was divine. Luckily roses in Malaysia blossom throughout the year because there are only two seasons: hot and raining. My mum would pick up the white rose in the morning and smell it a couple of times; then she'd stick it beautifully in her topknot. And sometimes my mum would spread them on her bed and the white rose would bring an overwhelming smell through all the night.

One bright hot afternoon my mum looked at the white roses; she wished the rain would pour down heavily just to shower all the white roses, but sadly it was sunny all day long. My mum couldn't wait for the afternoon to settle so she could pick her favourite white roses round the house. Anyway, the afternoon sun had settled down and my mum was already picking the white roses; she was so happy, her love growing with every white rose she picked. My mum was a very good woman; she never did any harm to anybody. She kept her problems to herself and I thank God for giving me this woman as my mum; no words can explain how much I love her.

Since I left my mum alone, as I promised, I gave her everything to give her the best life that she'd never had before. And in that time of my mum's life every morning when she woke up, she smiled like sunshine. I hope my mum received enough of what I gave to create great happiness in her life, and I am so blessed by God for being given the opportunity to show her how much I love and care for her. Actually, what my mum did for me, carrying me the whole twelve months in her stomach, was very hard and difficult. To bring me out to the world and to look after me was tough, and life was very challenging for her. Without my mum I would never be in this world and without my mum I wouldn't be who I am today. Thank you would never be enough, but she was the best mum ever. Now I understand that for my mum to be a mother for four children, especially without a husband, that is the hardest job in the world. Since that time my mum has always been in my thoughts, my prayers and in my heart with pure love. My mum was my life; I want to give her a full recovery from the pain that she'd had all her life. I wanted to keep my mum forever close throughout my life, but I knew that someday I'd have to let her go, and this was the hardest thing to accept in my entire life.

My Garden

In life the thing I most like to do is wake up early in the morning and refresh myself sitting outside in my garden before the sunrise strongly bursts. Every time I step out into my garden I feel like I've enter the garden of love – so my garden is secretly called, the garden of love. I love my garden because I'm surrounded with my favourite flowers and fruits, most of which I planted myself. I never get bored of looking at them, especially as they burst in the sun, bright in every corner of my garden, which makes my mind dance because of the natural creation. In every single plant that I planted my hand feels so much joy touching and flirting around with the soil, feeling that I gave the soil life to start. I take good care of my plants with so much pleasure and try as much as I can to allow them to live longer and never die.

Sometimes in the morning I decide to do almost nothing but sit in the summer house in my garden looking at all the many kinds of flowers; it just makes my heart and soul fill with so much of the greatest joy. To have this wonderful feeling and to see these marvellous views of

God's creation – it means that life is so perfect. My garden is a place for me to enjoy the beauty of life, especially seeing my favourite bird – the dove – fighting to eat its breakfast. The birdseeds in the bird feeder that I have hung on the branch of cherry blossom tree give me my happy morning. The doves climbing on top of each other just makes me giggle on my own. But they always stay close to each other, kissing their beaks and stroking their necks like a lovebird – absolutely beautiful to watch. I always notice that doves like to cry when they fly and wonder why, but the sound of crying really makes me sad. Anyhow, when they've had enough of eating the grey doves will fly out above and some of them cry, leaving me alone and leaving me with peace in my heart. I take my time to look at the natural beauty in my garden full of sunlight in every corner. Well, this is the best time of the day to say, 'Good morning to a beautiful morning, I will have a splendid day in my garden.' This glorious time of day is so precious for me, especially as the morning sunrise bursts in every tree in my garden.

Wow, the beautiful sunrise was out and started to warm my face and gently open my eyes wider; it just made me feel that this as a moment to enjoy in my life. I looked at the surroundings, all the greenery in my garden, with the radiant sunrise spreading upon nature; it was amazing, like a true work of art. I didn't know how long I would be sitting in the summer house, but my body started to get warm, especially as it was summertime. I stretched both my legs and closed my eyes; every time it takes my breath away, being so fresh in my lungs. I am truly blessed for my life each and every day. My eyes looked at the beautiful sunrise and smiled; with my soul I whispered, 'Life sometimes can be truly magical because at this moment I feel the world brings me a promise of life.' To see these spectacular sunrises burst, touching the earth, witnessing a creative God, I felt so alive. Slowly I took a sip of my favourite hot tea with raw honey which I have every morning after breakfast; it seemed to make my face burst with glowing. The most amazing thing was to see every day the sunrise greeting and kissing the earth, each time giving new life to the earth – absolutely breath-taking. This was one of the most spectacular events on earth that I had seen in all my life. My heart and soul smiled and said, 'Wow, no one can beat nature, and I feel like God's heart is in my garden.'

Anyway, I got up and slowly took a step, walking out from my summer house, then I stood at the corner of my garden while my eyes gently glanced at the morning sky; it made me feel so fresh. The clear blue sky calmed, and soft white running clouds felt like the magic of a morning promise for everything in life. I gently closed my eyes and my soul started with a prayer and with a positive thought, wishing myself to have a splendid day. Slowly I opened my eyes, looked at the sunshine and put a big smile on my face because my son Ryan always sings a song, 'You Are My Sunshine'. Not just that, he even calls me 'my sunshine' or 'my beautiful sunshine'; he is so adorable with all those words, absolutely take my breath away. Especially in the morning, when he opens his eyes he will say, 'I love you, my sunshine,' and is so beautiful; to hear that precious words in the morning just melts my heart, and I am the luckiest mother in the world. Suddenly I could feel soft morning winds blow on my face and gently play with my hair, feeling so fresh, cool and sweet. I could feel the winds, I could hear its sound and I could see all the leaves moving, touching the wind, but I couldn't say what it looked like. For me the winds, like a spirit, comes and whispers tenderly around you, then flies across the sky, across the land and the sea, and this amazing, beautiful scenery.

Suddenly a little robin bird flew from one tree to another, singing loudly with a beautiful melody, coming close to me and jumping up so friendly. I saw the same robin come in my garden every day, morning and evening. This little robin came close to me and joyfully sang; with smile I said, 'Good morning, little robin.' Oops, the robin quickly flew to another branch on my apple tree then to the cherry blossom. I love the red-breasted robin sitting on the cherry blossom, especially in the month of April as spring has arrived – absolutely beautiful. To hear the robin singing loudly on the cherry blossom tree made my heart so happy and brought me this joy on such a great morning. And to look at the happy robin jumping from one branch to another on the cherry blossom in this springtime, it's like a new life has begun. I love cherry blossoms, to see the pink flowers grow softly awake, singing deeply in my heart. So lovely and free, and it comes into bloom at the first promise of spring, especially glowing in the morning sun. What I love about the cherry blossom is that they grow quickly but then they don't last very long; sadly the season lasts for about a month.

Whoops! The little robin flew across my face and jumped inside the fountain in my garden with a flash and flicker of dripping wings. In my garden I have a big fountain and a few pretty little pools, and many kinds of birds walk and jump around, then stop to have a drink or have a bath. Anyhow, it put smile on my face and I couldn't take my eyes away from the little red-breasted robin waggling his tail, splashing and splashing, having a bath and singing loudly, nonstop. So astonishing to see so much beauty and nature in my garden; it brought me this joy on such a great morning.

I walked around in my garden then stopped, looking at the fence all along my garden, full of jasmine plants growing wild without stopping. The tiny flowers were very white, so bright and beautiful like a snowflake, and to see so many of them brought me such joy in my heart. But the scent of jasmine brought a smell the whole garden, so sweet and pure, filling my nose with such delight, and this was absolutely magical. Jasmine flowers' smell remind me of when I was a young girl, still living in the countryside, and my mum loved that particular flower called 'bunga melur'. The 'bunga melur' is small and very white, but the smell is of a heavenly perfume, exactly like jasmine flowers. My mum always asked me to pick them every morning and spread them all over on the bed, so fresh, and the smell was divine lasting all night long. My mum taught me a lot of things in life, and gave me the idea to do the same with jasmine flowers. Slowly the morning winds kissed my face and blew my hair; with my eyes closed it just made me feel so fresh and free. I took a deep breath, to my soul, smelling the sweet scent of jasmine flowers, and exhaled; it felt like the fragrance was letting me know of another morning to be remembered.

The morning sun was getting stronger, which made my body start to get warmer, so before I left my garden to start my beautiful day I gave a last look. Oh yes, my beautiful roses were in almost every corner, and they were blooming in my garden. I have red roses, pink roses, yellow roses, but my favourite rose is the white rose; it was one perfect rose, just reminding me of my mum. I'm pretty sure most women love red roses, especially those received from a loved one. Funnily enough I'm one of the women who don't like to receive roses because when the roses dry I have to chuck them in the bin – for me that's such a waste. I'd rather plant the rose myself and when the day comes the roses will continue to blossom, and that is what makes the spirit come alive. When I see the roses they always stay deep in my heart, and that moment I felt was one of the most magnificent times of my life. I looked up at the sky; a few birds flew high among the sky singing their wonderful tune, then I looked at all the roses, which grew like in heaven with love. Slowly I took footsteps towards the white rose sitting between the pink and red roses, also surrounded by lots of greenery. Straight away I stood in front of the white rose and gently touched the white rose; it felt so soft, the purest and sweetest, which took my breath away. And to see the white rose made me miss my mum dearly, especially as she was so far away from me. Well, the beauty of the white rose was like the beauty of my mum, which made my heart slowly whisper to me, saying, 'How I wish my mum was with me.' Again I gently touched the white rose in my mind; there were so many precious things about my mum that I needed to say. But the beauty of the white rose made me smile then I said, 'Mum, I miss you dearly and I'll send a guardian angel to look for you and to protect you always.'

Lastly I walked around and took a last look at my garden, all in bloom, and all the flowers and plants in my garden there are just like my friends. Well, it sounds a little crazy, but every time I look at them I smile, I talk with them and for me this is the most beautiful thing in my garden. Anyhow, after I had enjoyed a sweet time on my own, now it was time for me to walk away and leave my garden of love all alone.

During the Pandemic

The day that Covid-19 started was the day my mum's illness started; even though her memory was not hundred per cent, she still understood conversations with me. As I called my mum every day, finding whether she was well or not well was like a routine for me. With my mum's condition at that time, sometimes she remembered me, but most of the time she didn't, which broke my heart. And sometimes the most beautiful thing was when I had conversations with my mum about life and she responded beautifully with words; it made my heart smile. Honestly for fifty-seven years I always called her mum because she was my mum but never her name, Harisun; she would get mad with me. So then I going to test my mum by calling her by her name to see her reaction; if she got angry that would mean that she still remembered. Anyway, at 10am London time I called my brother to speak with my mum. The phone rang and my brother answered; after chatting for a few minutes with him he then passed the phone to my mum.

With so much confidence I asked my mum, 'Hello, Harisun, how are you?'

With a soft voice my mum responded, 'I am fine, who are you?'

I answered, 'I am your daughter, Izah.'

My mum just said, 'Oooo…'

Sadly my mum didn't remember me and she'd started to lose her memory; I was breaking down in tears. I held myself together and kept strong then continued to ask my mum, 'How are you doing?'

For some reason that morning I had a feeling that my mum wanted to talk; she then said, 'This morning is such a beautiful morning, the sun is shining bright and the birds are singing loud, so your brother has brought me outside the house to get some morning sun.'

I replied, 'Wow, that's fantastic, and yes, morning sun is good for you, Mum.' I asked her again, 'Are you sitting on the swing or on the chair?'

With her tender voice my mum replied, 'Sitting in the wheelchair on my own, I stretch my hand and my whole body feels such relief, but I feel my life is so empty. I want to talk to everyone but sometimes my mouth locks and doesn't allow me to open it – I don't know for what reason.'

To hear all those sentences, my heart was crying so sadly, then I said, 'I understand, Mum, but you always can talk to me.'

I could hear her sweet tiny laugh and my mum replied, 'This morning for the first time I feel my life is missing something and at the same I feel my whole body is gone forever from my life. However I am so lucky that I'm still alive so I will try to get better – I just hope everything going to be fine.'

To hear my mum saying all those words broke my heart badly; I wished I could jump on the plane straight away and be with her. 'Please God, make my mum better and save her life; all I want is happiness for my mum' – so many thoughts ran through my head. I hoped the fresh morning made my mum build the fresh beginning of her new life. My mum was still sitting outside in the sun but she started to slow down and stop talking. I tried to make some joke to make her laugh but she was still silent so I just said goodbye to her. I could feel my mum's heart was full of sadness. At the same time I was really worried and scared of the pain continuing to damage my mum's life. But I was very proud of my mum because the beautiful side of her is that she had a very strong mind, which made her think that she needed to say goodbye to all the fear in her life and just let the past be.

At this stage my conversation with my mother was like one with a stranger because she couldn't remember me anymore. However in our conversation I always promised her that as soon as everything was back to normal the first thing that I was going to do was fly back to see her. But then I couldn't change the situation; the worst feeling ever that I didn't know when this pandemic was going to end. Especially every day seeing that the cases were high and more people were dead; it was so scary, what was happening round the world. The news I watched left me emotional and in pain. Especially as you couldn't say goodbye when a loved one died – that would be the worst feeling in the world. I was alone, didn't feel much like talking to anyone about the situation back home, but

I always had huge questions inside my mind. The most serious thing was that no aeroplane could fly: 'Wow, how can I go home to see my mum?' Well, now another question I needed to know the answer to: 'How long is this coronavirus going to last?' I tried to get the answers myself, but it made my feelings so low and drained me completely. However, I was concerned and worried about my mum when I thought about the coronavirus taking people's life. At the same time I wished I had the power of magic so I could destroy this coronavirus and save the world. I also wished and prayed to God that my mum would get better and back to her normal life so I could teach her how to spread her wings and learn to fly again. I was heartbroken to know that my mum had had a stroke and one side of her body was paralysed. Slowly I closed my eyes and my soul whispered to the angel then made a wish to save my mum's life and for me to be able to see her.

All those conversations between myself and my mum made my heart, each morning when I opened my eyes, worry about her and think about her. I was on the other side of the world and across the ocean I could see my mum's sadness, but I hoped her life would continue to be bright. For me I had to keep myself strong, as life is too short, so I would continue to live each day with appreciation; of course I would always pray for my mum to make sure she was getting better every day. The most beautiful thing in my life was to pray for my mum every day, and with blessings of happiness I could do my things in peace. Deep in my heart I always felt the journey of conversations between myself and my mum continuing with one love but two hearts as I missed her dearly. I expressed my feelings with three powerful magic words – 'I love you' – to my mum. And these magic words I hoped would touch her deep in her soul and full promising make her life smile of love with liquid of joy.

I rested my back on the chair, tied my hair, made a little ponytail, freshened my face, freshened my mind. Today my mum made me feel more alive after I managed to have a little conversation with her. And today my prayer for my mum was that I hoped she had a beautiful day and really hoped she could start her brand-new life. Well, with her condition it was very difficult to predict but miracles can happen. From now was the time for me to start to focus and do everything that I could to be able to go home to see her before it was too late. At the same time I would try to give my mum freedom to make the most of it while she still could enjoy life.

However, I was very proud of my brother Ridzwan, who dressed up my mum beautifully every day even though she didn't talk, but I am sure she buried her emotions deep inside her soul. And my brother Zambri, who always tried to keep my mum strong and talk to her. but I knew for sure in her mind that she worried if this pain would ever go away. And my little sister Nurul, always there when everyone needed help, and she always looked at all my mum's sadness but then turned away and hid the key in a secret place in her life. Sadly with myself far away I couldn't do anything for my mum but I made sure to look after every single one of my siblings, keeping them in a good place with finances, and to look after my mum; this duty was like part of my life for my family. All of us really took good care of our mum and the world with fake smiles but living pain in our heart. Luckily with technology nowadays I always received pictures and videos of my mum that my siblings have WhatsApped me. My mum always smiled with her new image. I hoped she would not just have a smile on her face today; but I hoped she would smile tomorrow, next week, next month, next year, with a continuing smile for the rest of her life.

I took a deep breath and whispered in my heart, 'Mum, I am very sorry for not being there when you needed me.' Without words this was hurting me badly but now I was going to keep all my sadness in one corner of my heart. As much as I would love to be with my mum, because of Covid I had to forget about travelling at the moment, especially as the country went into lockdown. With Covid I felt like the world was changing, making peoples move on to start a fresh new chapter of life. Luckily for me I felt life had to have experiences, and this experience would teach me to be a stronger person and think positively. But I wouldn't wait for long; please, God, take me to be with my mum so I can help my mum rebuild her life. Especially as my mum had already started talking and managed to have a conversation with me even though she didn't know who I as. But thanks to God; as time went along my mum started to enjoy conversations, talk about life and start to remember her siblings, which was a big step for her and every one of us. With my mum's improvement I felt her smile back again; it brought so much joy to my life. Every single time, to hear my mum laugh would take my pain away and to be able to talk to her made my soul start to dance around. My mum's tender and gentle voice made my heart melt and wiped my sadness away. I had not managed to have a proper conversation with my mum for such a very long time. Even though we were both far away from each other, listening my mum's voice be almost back to normal I felt close to her in my heart. Only my soul whispered to my mum that I loved and missed her so much. But my mum still had to find the key by herself to build her life back; of course with the help of my two brothers and sister. From now my happiness was like a butterfly the more I breeds the more happiness I have in my life which makes me dream with loving memories. Without noticing tears overwhelming me, running down my cheeks, full butterflies were in my stomach flying happily. At 9pm I was standing in my garden so I looked up at the clear sky while the full moon showed me what a miracle life is.

I am very grateful to my siblings, who took really good care of our mum, and surely that special care brought wonderful things to my mum's life since the day she became unwell. I hoped and was pretty sure that every time my mum opened her eyes she could see the beauty of love from her children. Especially my two brothers, who took turns to clean her, wash her and feed her – not an easy job. But both of them did so without pressure, full of energy, care and big smile. All they did made my mum be full of happiness in her heart, which made her world full of love and peace. To have a family like that, I couldn't ask for more other than blessings, and I was sure my mum had lifetime happiness. I maybe didn't know how hard is was to look after my mum, but both of my brothers and my sister had told me of their experiences well enough to make me understand how difficult what they been through was. My heart hurt badly for them; I wished I was there to look after my mum. But I had a difficult time too: to support every single one of them and finance taking care of my mum. But that bloody Covid made life unfair and made me feel so guilty. At that moment there was nothing more I wanted in the world other than just to be with my mum because she needed me. Anyhow, I am so proud of my siblings; they had grown quicker than I expected so with them care making my destiny. The care that they gave to our mum brought me to tears with happiness and no words can describe how much I love them all. It meant a lot to me even though we just spent time on the phone, but it brought me so much closer. I couldn't ask for a better life, so thank you to all of you for looking after our mum.

It's fresh in my mind and will always be in my mind forever: at the beginning her illness she said, 'Mum will pray for you to come home, but if you can't, Mum understands. Just look after yourself and Mum will pray for your life always.'

Since my mum said those words each morning when I opened my eyes my heart worried about her and thought about her badly. I was on the other side of the world and crossed many oceans; I could see my mum's sadness but I hoped her life would continue to be bright. For me I had to keep myself strong for my mum and pray for her every day for God to save her life. The beautiful thing in life was to pray for my mum every day, and with my happiness, which made me live in peace. Deep in my heart I always felt the journey of conversations between myself and my mum continued with one love but two hearts, as I was missing her dearly.

From then the precious time that I waited for every day was to happily talk to my mum as soon as I woke up – so looking forward to hearing her voice. It's been almost more than a year since my mum has been able to walk. Sometimes my mum felt that she was a burden to her children. My mum didn't notice that the words that she was saying were hard for us to take and really hurtful. What my mum didn't know was that the best thing in our life was to look after her. Especially my brother Ridzwan, who stayed with my mum, always woke up in the middle of the night to clean my mum then looked at my mum's face until she was peacefully asleep. And my brother Zambri too sometimes came around and stayed overnight, looking after my mum all night. I have no words to describe how appreciative I am to both of them; the way they cared for my mum was absolutely amazing. Slowly I closed my eyes, and prayed, prayed and prayed, hoping that my mum would recover from sickness quicker – that was all I can do. I couldn't tell anyone, not even my siblings, how much devastating pain was inside me, and my heart was beating so weakly, almost torn to pieces, thinking about my mum. Sometimes I tried to ignore it, not thinking about it a lot, but the behaviour of my brain really burned from the pain. Instead I secretly cried in my heart. And sometimes I just wanted to get out from the house and try to keep myself busy, but my mum's condition left me without energy and power to do anything. Especially I understood how much my mum was in pain, suffering, and it hurt; that was why I needed to be with her at that moment. But I had done everything in my power to look after my siblings and my mum to make sure they received a good life from me. I would not allowed them to struggle or be in deep pain; this is how much I care about my family. Anyway, with all the suffering to think about my mum which make my heart and soul become frozen and no fire to milky out. Day by day I cried from the pain, and the longer I left it the more the sadness grew, creating the most hurt and suffering, which left my life surrounded in darkness.

This coronavirus was happening everywhere, all over the world, like a natural war which kept taking people's life until the country had to lock down. Maybe some people enjoyed the lockdown, but I didn't, especially as I couldn't fly back home to see my mum with her illness. Well, I did understand and I knew I had to accept and needed to face the fact that this was our life for now, but not going on for nearly two years. This coronavirus walked over our lives, became like an evil power, thriving and thriving – how nasty was this virus.

For two good months my mum got better and was able to have good conversations with every one of us, but of course some of the stuff was very funny, which she didn't know what she talking about. I kept laughing nonstop; it was hilarious, but she made my heart so cheerful. Sometimes my mum remembered me but then within a second she forgot who I was. Funny enough, most of the time my mum called me 'Sister Zah'; she thought I was her sister. I was very happy with whatever she called me as long as she was getting better; that was more important. But out of the blue one evening my mum was not feeling too well; suddenly she collapsed. The ambulance had come and taken my mum to hospital; God knew how worried I was with my stomach starting to get cramps thinking about what had happened to my mum. With there being different times between London and Malaysia, it was so difficult for me to ask for more information about my mum. It was night time in Malaysia ,so I let them sleep while I worried and patiently waited for tomorrow.

I didn't sleep all night and my hand kept holding the phone just in case they called me to tell me about my mum. It was the next day at nine in the morning London time that I received magical news from my sister Nurul that my mum could return home. I was over the moon – thank God. This magical news made my dreams come true; it was simply beyond words and tears of happiness ran down my cheeks. From far away my heart couldn't stop smiling and the happiness that I felt from my mum's news was the privilege of my life at that moment. I just imagined that soon I would sit beside my mum and hold her arms, and if this happened that would be one of the magnificent gifts of my life. Anyhow, my mind started to worry again because since she'd returned home from hospital she'd stopped talking. And the bad news was that my mum was not able to eat or drink through her mouth. My mum only drank special milk from a tube through her nose. This upset me, broke my heart, especially as I couldn't hear her voice anymore, nor her laughing and joking; that news made my brain completely blocked.

After a week with my mum out from hospital I still was not able to hear her voice, then I started to realise her life was in a bad stage. Most of the time my mum kept silent, not a word coming out of her mouth. Day by day my mum's condition did not get any better; it just made me cry day and night, thinking about how my mum's life would never be the same again. Almost every day I looked at myself in the mirror to see how much stress was showing in my face, thinking of the pain and suffering that my mum had been through. My tears dried out from crying every day while my heart and soul were damaged to thinking of how much longer my mum could live. But please, God, give my mum more life to live in this world, and please, God, take me home to be with my mum. The only prayer I did was for my mum, hoping the pain and suffering that she'd received would soon be over.

My mind was screaming, full of anger; the whole world could hear how upset I was with this pandemic happening round the world. But sadly, my mind was just on my own and felt so much pain about the situation at the moment. Only my tears accompanied me, but I was crying without a sound, which made my anger build with so much hatred for Covid, which didn't care or take responsibility. Even though where I was now was a thousand miles away from my country, the distance could never change the anger I felt inside my heart. At this moment I let my mind fly high with the wind for a refresh then returned full of energy. Even though the clouds came flooding into my life, I no longer had to carry rain or bring a storm and colour into my life. For me life was one big road with lots of signer and never complicated my smile flee from hate. Whatever I did in life, I had to have trust and confidence, but I didn't bury my thoughts and make my vision into reality. This was the sadness in my life; to think that for two long years my mum had her illness and for two years I couldn't go back to see her, killed me badly inside. The most hurtful thing was when my mum started to lose her memory; it just felt like someone stabbed my heart. Every day I was in pain and the pain was getting worse until it was buried deep in my soul. Suddenly my brain interrupted and I became angry again, thinking about when this pandemic was going to end. And my tears ran down warmly, thinking about all those unlucky people, their life taken by Covid for nothing. Sometimes we need little tears to clear the mist in our eyes and a little announce to clear the doubts in our head this is what just happen to me. At this moment it was nice if I had a little hug from someone to comfort my heart and to lend me a shoulder to cry on.

Time had gone so fast already, the pandemic still jumping high; it was the same with my mum's condition, not getting any better. I just didn't know what to do. On Sunday evening I just entered the house coming back from a day out; suddenly I received a call from my brother Zambri saying through tears that my mum had been taken to hospital again to save her life but this time she was seriously ill. I only felt my body with me in London but my heart and my soul was in Malaysia with my mum just holding tight for her life. I only had to wait for my siblings to update me about my mum's situation, but while I was waiting my heart was burning with fire, with anger at life thinking that life is unfair. And my question was why did this have to happen right now at this time, which I would never have expected in my entire life. All night I couldn't sleep thinking about my mum; it felt like a nightmare. My mum spent more than a week in the hospital, and thank God that he saved her life again. But this time it was really hard work for my siblings because my mum needed full care, and it was harder for me to handle everything from a far.

I started calling her name since she was not well and not herself, just to refresh her memory so she did not forget who she was. I always looked at the sunny side of life, the ups and the downs, the truth of a beginning; we need water to grow and we need seeds to sow. The same thing is in human life: some of the things have to change and some of the things have to be done. For what I see today is bringing us more for tomorrow and award for thing in life. And almost every single day my mind couldn't stop thinking of what was happening round the world with the coronavirus. What as most scary was that if you got it you were either alive or dead; this was like horror. Even now a lot of them being showered all their heart that their burred. My heart is with everyone who's lost a loved one, and I pray for God to bless them every day with the softest rain, like April showers, to bring them the loveliest things in May.

Nasty Covid-19

On 28 March 2022 this time my mum was very ill; my siblings called an ambulance and she was admitted to hospital. I started to get very worried, especially as Covid cases were still high in Malaysia, and with my mum's condition my heart was shaking for her. Because during the night in Malaysia, as it was also during Covid, all my siblings were not allowed to be with my mum. We were given no choice but to have to wait: a stressful day for me in London and a stressful night for my siblings in Malaysia. At night I never went bed before performing my prayer and after my prayer I usually went straight to bed. But that night the time was a bit earlier than usual so I decided to rest myself on the lonely bed in the silent night, and for some reason my mind was thinking about my mum. I opened the window get some fresh air but it looked like entire world seemed to be fast asleep. And when I looked at my window all the trees waved at me, so I guess only they awakened from their sleep. And I was wondering why life can sometimes be very sad. But then when I blinked my eyes, my mind ran faster, just thinking about my mum's life. It brought sad thoughts to my mind, that this might be the last day for my mum to stay on this earth; if so, I didn't know how to accept it.

The next day in hospital my mum was being examined by the doctor while I was waiting nervously for news from any one of my siblings. At the same time my mind comforted myself, thinking that my mum would be fine. Suddenly my sister Nurul called me; my heart pumped so fast, almost going to explode. I was so scared and worried about what kind of news she was going to deliver to me about my mum. I was on the phone with my sister waiting nervously; she then said, 'Sis, I don't how to say this, but Mum has Covid.'

With so much sadness I told my sister, 'Just pray for Mum and update me with whatever news you have about her,' and we both were in tears finishing our conversation. The day was still sunny with the leaves just turning glory and for the skies of couple colour as a brindled cow but the world is not conclusion. A species stood beyond with my mind full, thinking about the condition of my mum. And my mind imagined that I heard her voice screaming like thunder, asking where I was. My heart could hear my mum's voice crying like music from the moon, needing the caring hand of her daughter. I tried to comfort myself from these sad feelings by listening to the sweet birds. But my heart ached and a drowsy numbness pained me with every minute that passed and wards had sunk. Sometimes I feel like a dream but the hand of God I promise of my own life and pray hope life back to normal so I be able to go back to be with her. I believed in my soul and believed in my words that things would get better soon. But if I still couldn't go home I just wanted my mum's life to go back to normal, then I would be happy, seeing her fly, a flock of beating wings.

It was 29 March 2022 when my sister and brothers told me that our mum was infected with Covid. As soon as I heard the word Covid my whole system was in shock; I almost fainted. I never expected that Covid would get my mum. Again I felt my heart burning like a wildfire with anger at this virus; there were so many questions in my head. I was on my own, didn't know what to do, and my brain was completely blank; I couldn't think of anything but anger at this bloody nasty Covid. With my broken heart and with a prayer for my mum, I walked round my bedroom, forward and backward, like a stressed tiger in a cage. This Covid really turned lives – for myself, my family and people around the world – upside down.

After a few hours I received a call from my siblings that my mum was on oxygen; she was struggling to breathe; the disease spreading fast around my mum's body. God knew how scared I was and my body started to tremble, which was hard to stop, just hoping that God would save my mum's life. It really broke my heart in two. My mum was sick; I couldn't go back to be with her, wash her, dress her or feed her. Especially that I couldn't talk to her, laugh with her, touch her skin and just spend precious time with her. But at this stage I was begging God, 'Please and please give my mum time to live so I can see her.' I hoped God would listen to me.

That evening I didn't feel like eating anything but instead I decided to sit in my garden, kept company by the lonely night. It was very strange; I felt everything was weird, but the night kept me alive even though I knew anything could happen to my mum's life. Gently I took a deep breath and, looking at the night sky, I said, 'Please, God, save my mum's life. If my mum goes, I've lost the friend who I always talk to about everything – it would be so difficult for me to build my life without her.' Suddenly my adorable son Ryan softly put his hands around my body and kissed me over and over without noticing my tears warmly touching my cheeks. Then my son said, 'Mummy, I love you, you are my life and my sunshine.' To hear those beautiful words helped me bring back the happiness and joy to my life. There was nothing more I can do than just love him; he is my world.

With a big smile I grasped my son's hand and said, 'Your hugs make Mummy warm and take Mummy out of this sadness at this moment, and you have given Mummy enough to remind her of when you were a baby – that brightened up Mummy. *Tu es ma cherie et tu es mon coeur heart*,' as I always say to him with French words.

I felt so tired waiting for the phone call, and to make my body wake up I gently massaged my head to feel more alert. The night was still young; there was just silence in the night around me. I looked up at the sky, the moon moving softly, surrounded by a thousand stars. I could imagine that my mum was having a difficult time in her life at that moment. I felt so heartbroken knowing that when people got Covid, they would either live or die. I tried not to think much about it, again looking at the moon, so beautiful but sadly far away from me, just like my mum being far away from me. My mum is my soul; she is always close to my heart. I then whispered to myself, 'God! In my life I have found everything I want, but now I am asking you to save my mum's life. She is my whole world so please don't take her without me seeing her.' My eyes looked at the moon and stars, hoping that the beautiful moon would bring me some blessings and a beautiful message. But deep down inside me I was full of sadness and bitterness to know that my mum would die sooner or later; it could be that night, could be tomorrow night or could be in my dream. My eyes were so weak, and I'd completely lost my strength, but I pushed myself to get up.

The silent night got a bit sad and the stars lit up one by one, the moon still looking down on me. In the dark I was in tears, but the power of Covid made me angry, full of energy to continue, whispering, 'I am very sorry, Mum, that Covid entered your life.' Soon I left my garden peacefully and entered the house.

I didn't sleep all night, especially as London, United Kingdom, is seven hours behind Malaysia. Wait, wait and wait. Suddenly at 3am I received a call from all my siblings that the doctor had told them to be ready as my mum could go at any time. To hear that news my body became like a statue; I couldn't even cry, as my tears were frozen, and I couldn't even scream, as my voice was lost somewhere. To comfort my soul, to calm down my heart from more breaking and to give me peace, I decided to pray for my mum while waiting for the phone call. Honestly, I could feel that I was not going to see my mum forever. And I knew that my sad time was not far away, maybe a second or a minute away. I tried not to cry out and not to scream but I couldn't lock the pain away, as suddenly my tears ran out without notice. Anyway, I closed my eyes with a prayer. I could see my mum's beautiful smile, I could see her wave goodbye then slowly disappear in heaven in peace. Just a second after I finished my prayer I missed a call from my sister missed then from my brothers. Gosh, this was the first time in my entire life that I'd been so scared but I prepared for the worst. Quickly I returned my sister's call; within a second she answered and said, 'Hello, sis, I am so sorry but Mum is dead.'

It was 4am London time on Wednesday 30 March 2022 and this date will be programmed in my brain for the rest of my life. I knew it was going to happen this way, but her sudden unexpected death within three days was shocking to my whole world. The loss of my mum really broke my heart; I couldn't hold her hand, hug her, comfort her, especially through her sickness, and now she'd died alone in hospital. How I wished that I could be with my mum as she took her last breath. And the words died, bring me to silence; after a few seconds my body was completely weak, no words, can speaking, no voice to scream, only warm tears running down my cheek without stopping; then I said to my sister, 'I will speak with you later.'

Soon I ended the conversation with my sister, my legs shaking, hardly able to stand. Slowly I sat on the chair thinking my mum was no longer with me. I didn't know how to get over the loss of my mum but I had to learn how to live with it. It was hard for me to accept that my mum was gone forever from me and from this world, and I'd lost my first and forever friend. My eyes flooded with tears and my heart hurt badly thinking how cruel it was for life to take my mum away from me forever. I am so appreciative that my mum waited for me for two years, but God loved her more than me because she suffered. The day Covid started, that was the day my mum fell sick. I felt like it was a dream, and I still thought my mum was still alive and she was still waiting for me. Suddenly I heard the birds singing in my garden; slowly I got up, walked to the window. I can see a few doves sitting on the branch of the cherry blossom tree, waiting for me to feed them breakfast. I looked up at the morning sky and started to scream loud, like I was hysterical, and was given all my power by my guilt from not seeing my mum. At the same time as I was looking at the pictures of my mum, my sister Nurul WhatsApped me. I saw the final picture of my mum's face – she looked so beautiful and peaceful, her body lying like a piece of wood, still and sweet. God made my mum so she would never grow old. My mum's cheekbones were still fresh-faced like a white rose and made me think I just wanted to grow old and be like her. My poor mum; she was just a countryside girl many years ago and she had told me about her dream to be a lawyer. Sadly her dream didn't come true. Most of the time my mum was all alone but this time she would be alone forever inside the earth. Yet my heart was broken because I couldn't understand why someone so precious had to die and now she was going to sleep forever. I continued to look at my mum's picture; gently my soul whispered, 'I know you can't hear my voice but your spirit will. Just to let you know, I love you, Mum, and always will do. I will miss you forever in my life and always will.'

As spring came round the corner the sunlight burst early, bright, and danced on the air everywhere. Before I closed the window I looked at my white roses waving goodbye to March and goodbye to my mum, who had died at the end of March. Tomorrow would be another day, but the day after tomorrow is springtime. I stood still and wept; it hurt to think that my mum had left me without a word. I felt so weak, especially to hear doves crying at the end of March. My wish for the month of April was for it to erase all my sadness. I gave a last look at the white roses and with my heart whispered, 'Sleep well, Mum, and dream of May when you are in heaven.'

The month of March is the month that I so look forward to because March has just blown in with smile to say that spring will soon begin. But in the year 2022 the month of March was the saddest month because my mum had breathed her last breath and would never return. So I quickly went in the garden just to spend more time in the early morning in my garden while hearing the winds of March whisper in my ears that spring was just round the corner. Sometimes it can be slightly chilly in the morning but the winds of March worked to keep blowing the winter cold away. The morning was so bright and I could feel the spring in the air, but I was so happy the longer nights had ended. Nature makes me enjoy the season of spring so much; it brings me so much happiness and a joyful time. Seeing some of the flowers smiling at me with the wind, March joyfully playing with hair, I just hoped this month would bring something new in my life.

As my siblings were not allowed to wash or dress my mum for the last time, they just waited for the hospital to get my mum ready. It was so painful to stare at my mum's picture. I closed my eyes with tears rolling straight to my heart and again whispered to my mum's spirit, saying, 'Mum, I know you can't feel my tears and I know you can't hear my crying tone, but your leaving me all of a sudden has torn me inside badly. My life now is not the same without you around, Mum.'

As a Muslim my mum had to be buried the same day, so after a few hours I received a video of my mum's funeral from my sister Nurul. Luckily all my siblings were allowed to go to the funeral but was heartbreaking seeing all my siblings sitting six feet apart; it was so awful that they only managed to see the coffin. And for myself, on the other side of the world with my heavy heart, tears flooded in my eyes to see the video of them laying my mum to rest and saying our last goodbyes. I am so grateful for technology; now from afar I will be able to see her graveyard, full of sadness. I am so lucky to have such a beautiful mum, but I am not lucky to lose her at a very early stage. Who am I going to find to replace my mum because there will never be another mum in this world who can be like my mum. The special thing about my mum and myself was that we had a very special bond and secret to share like a best friend forever. Even though my mum means so much to me, I was still losing her and she left me a beautiful memory, and no one can displace my memories with her. The hardest thing in my life was to lose her, but I couldn't thank my mum enough for being my lifelong friend.

Anyhow, this trauma of Covid has changed how we live and die, and has changed funerals too. To lose my mum because of Covid was very painful and traumatic for me and the rest of my family, especially with not being able to see our mum's funeral.

From now my mum has left me with all the things which remind me of my mum's wicked laugh; it bring my knees together in place. All those memories between myself and my mum bury me, but she had to bear a lot of pain. As soon as my mum was infected with Covid I always knew that sooner later she would die but I hoped she'd stay a little longer and wait for me; sadly there was no miracle this time. After I watched the video funeral of my mum I took steps walking slowly to the window, looked up at the morning sky with my heart pounding and my tears pouring nonstop, thinking how fast she'd gone. At that moment it took time for me to accept the reality of my mum's death. From a thousand mile away I was saying goodbye to my mum's body but it was not easy, so I tried to think all the happiness myself and my mum had shared. But what hurt even more was to see the difficulty my mum had in blowing her last breath without any one of her children around her. However, a million thank-yous for the hospital, who made a video call so that all my siblings were able to see my mum. My brothers and sister comforted my mum with a few words before her last moments of life, so she would hear all those beautiful messages from her children. Anyhow, I could feel my mum's soul still with me, but now God let her free from all the pain that she'd suffered, bless her heart. Before I walked away from the window I finally looked up to the sky and the glorious sun smiled towards me. If I had one wish I would ask that the sun would bring back my mum's life but that was impossible. Even though my life was no longer present, my soul and my mum's soul would never part. So I took one last look at the video of my mum's funeral and the picture of her while my heart whispered, 'Sleep well, Mum, and I love you very much, more than the full moon or the beautiful star in the night sky. Come to my dreams every night and tell me the story about how you met an angel in heaven. Goodbye, Mum, I'll see you in heaven.'

Later in the afternoon, I only spoke with all my siblings but didn't feel like talking to anyone else, which left me so heartbroken, so I decided to sit in my garden. All of a sudden I could feel a few drops of rain on my face; it made me awake but I ignored the rain. This was just because my mind kept going on thinking about going back to Malaysia to visit my mum's graveyard. But I still had to be aware of Covid; however I always had my secret thoughts that I kept in my soul. I did my little part to pray for the right thing to do at this moment. With my heart bright like the sun I prayed for the beautiful white rose to be brought to heaven, which never dies. I have so much anger wrapped around my heart with Covid, leaving a hole in my heart, until I felt my warm blood running fast in my body. Suddenly my tears drizzled down my cheekbones as I bit my soft lips to avoid anger. But then I thought, this world is too sad for tears and I would not weep, so I smiled along with a broken heart. The sky was blue when I was out in the garden but now the clouds gathering had turned very dark and I was very scared. I was so happy at the end of March, looking forward for April, but then my world had been ripped apart. With my cry I left all the pain out and I screamed without a sound, just wandered lonely as a cloud. And I was still sitting under the tree, looking at the dark clouds which were going to send more rain, then I thought, 'It's time to run.' By that time it was too late; the dark clouds had rolled over and the raindrops hit me and the ground hard. I was rushing to get up but then I stood and let the rain shower me; it was April showers. My eyes clouded from the rainy spell; my hair was wet and my clothes were soaking wet. I felt so much better. As I'd been in England such a long time I was already used to the English weather. I walked around in my garden, stepping and kicking in the puddles; it splashed some happiness which made me feel so wonderful, the rain in springtime. The smell of the earthy soil that had been hit by the rain cleansed my soul; I felt so sensational. How I love this unique smell, with this magic rain in spring. I feel so pure and glorious, like my new life has just grown in the earth. Everywhere showing me the beauty a moment is born it only seen in the springtime. To hear the joy of many kinds of birds whistling to each other brings magnificent memories of my mum. But my eyes admired and appreciated nature in the springtime.

Soaking wet, I walked in the house and cleaned and dried myself. Of course my mum was all over my mind as I slowly brought myself to sit at my antique chair and thanked my favourite springtime that had given me so much strength which I needed at that moment. I rested my heart and soul while I enjoyed the evening settling down, but as the day got longer the sun was still so bright. But I felt so tired of the pain, thinking about the loss of my mum and the hurt in my soul when she went unexpectedly. My mind circled like a clock, nonstop thinking about how fast Covid had taken her life. This nasty Covid left my body completely drained; at the end of the day I'd only had a little joy.

Anyhow, the evening was so calm and I felt my body inviting me to rest for longer, so I decided to be with my mum's soul for the rest of the evening. With joy in my eyes I looked at the sun moving down and the evening wind slowly settling. My heart was full of a smile while my eyes let the evening go on, then I thought, 'This is the perfect time for me to listen to a little music.' I got up and looked at my CD collection; my favourite music is country music. So I decided to listen to 'When the Sun Goes Down', sang by Kenny Chesney. Honestly, I listened to every single word and I felt like someone had whispered to my heart with beautiful words that no one could ever say; it was a splendid moment. Also this song reminded me of two things my mum had constantly told me when I was a teenager: one was to be a good woman, which I am now, and the other was don't give up in life just like her. I am so lucky to have had a mother who taught me to become so independent and a fighter for everything in life. Even though since I was a teenager I left my mum to go to a different city to try and find some extra money to help my mum. But I'll never throw away what she taught me, no matter where she is, in heaven or here on earth. It became part of my life until I am today still following her rule of life which is nobody can do the thing that she does for me.

From the bottom of my heart I thank my mum for the million things she has done for me as I always did and appreciated when she was still alive. I am sure my mum knew I always thought about her, especially when we were far away, and to make sure I listened to her voice every single day. Especially now she was gone, I thought of my mum a million times, and life without her would never be the same. And sadly my mum was no longer with me to listen to her beautiful sweet voice. I'll miss my mum in a million ways, of course – the way our chatting went on for hours and hours, gossiping about people nonstop. But sometimes some of conversation ended with arguments because of some disagreement and we both hung up the phone. The next day we both went back to normal again – yesterday is gone and today is a new day – but sometimes this could go on for a week and this was how I shared my time with my mum. All those secrets with a million moments that my mum and myself shared from when I was born until her death, forever in my heart. Only God knows how heartbroken I am to lose her as a mother and as my best friend in this world. But the most important thing is that I loved my mum for a million reasons, some she'd never know until I meet her again up above in heaven.

At this moment what makes my soul run to my thoughts and makes me think is to travel right now because of the Covid. Especially sitting in the plane for thirteen hours without stopping, it just makes me very frustrating. Why did this Covid have to happen? I held my anger in my heart and it felt like my entire world had fallen apart. Every time I thought that Covid had taken my mum's life, it was very painful and hurt my soul badly and left a scar right to the bone. Honestly, since Covid had taken my mum's life and since that time my mind had never stopped thinking about it. I then slowly whispered and comforted myself and prayed for God to save people's lives around the world. Each day I thought about how Covid had taken my mum's life; it hurt, even deeper, with floods of tears like a pool. I made my prayer every day, hoping this pandemic would be over and we could return to a normal life very soon.

Suddenly my stomach started to make noise and I started to get hungry even though I didn't feel like eating but I had to grasp something to fill up my stomach. I was having a very light dinner: smoked salmon with salad while the music went on; in fact it went on all night long. Suddenly I felt the cool wind blowing fresh into my face; it prompted my brain to look at the time – wow, it was midnight but my soul was still feeling sad in the midnight spring wind. Quickly I jumped in the bed and hid my body under my soft blue cotton covers while my heart was filled with joy to think that my mum was resting in peace in heaven. And to think that I would be able to return home to visit my mum's graveyard and that moment was spectacular. My mum is my life and my whole world; I couldn't wait for the day that I could stand in her graveyard. It just felt like a precious gift given to me from heaven far above, but it would be in my soul for days, weeks and years, and here I am, your daughter.

Gosh! My sleep time had passed, but I was still awake trying to count days and weeks, even months holding off my impatience at knowing about my son's school holiday so I could fly back home. To see my mum's graveyard would give me so much happiness. That feeling I'd never had in my entire life and no explanation to express myself. But from now every day I could only dream, thinking how beautiful my mum looked when she smiled. Most of all I so much looked forward to touching the soil in my mum's graveyard and to lay the white rose and to talk with her spirit. I love to feel that feeling but of course the main concern was keeping myself healthy and away from any virus. My mum was a very independent and caring person with a heart of diamond. Well, there are so many more good things about my mum that I can talk about, which never end, but all those are in my prayers. Only God knows what my brain has in store. Every time I want to think about my mum I will lay on my bed at midnight because that is the time that is so peaceful when I fall asleep. All the memories of myself and my mum come to my life like an angel and give me so much beauty in my soul. I think of my mum, how funny she was, which just makes my heart giggle nonstop, and that feeling is beyond the world. Especially in the spring night, I glow when I think about my mum. Anyway, I can't wait until I am at my mum's graveyard, to tell her, 'I am sorry, Mum, that I was not with you when you were ill and not with you when you blew your last breath. But I am the proudest daughter in the world because since I was a little girl I looked after you, helping you around, giving you happiness and making you smile, giving you everything in life and I never stopped looking after you until the day you died, and I am so honoured to be your daughter; with all my heart I love you very much.'

Goodbye White Rose

In this book, *Goodbye White Rose*, I am writing down some beautiful stories of my mum and her soul. It was the month of April, and April is the month of showers and brings a May flower – that is what they say, but I am sure there is meaning behind the words. But then if all the showers have turned to flowers I'm pretty sure we'd have quite a colourful day. And this was the perfect time for me to start doing things in life because April onwards bring me so much sadness in my life at this moment. However I am so grateful that I managed to start writing the story of my mum to comfort my own heart but most of the time tears were running down my cheeks. It was very sad and painful because my mum was no longer with me, but my soul gave me so much strength to believe in myself and to continue with life. Some paragraph that I have written about my mum I need more oxygen to breathe. My mum is my world, my life, my soulmate; I can't believe she has gone without me beside her; I felt like my world had shut down completely. From a little girl I've looked after my mum and never stopped looking after her until the day of her last breath.

The next day in the morning I was in my garden because I love morning and I love to say good morning to the morning which makes me feel so great for the rest of the day. Especially feeling the morning mist kisses; it makes my whole body and soul freshly awake. And also the morning mist kiss the one make my heart smiling bright with full of joy. Honestly each time I kissed the morning mist I feel another year younger and I feel my face sparkle like stars. But sadly the morning didn't last long like afternoon and evening, so I would spend my time well for the rest of the morning. As soon as the sun was out it started to dry out the morning mist on my face; suddenly I heard the birds on the trees all singing to welcome the light. Thoughts crossed my mind that if I were a bird I would fly high happily without worrying about anything in life. Flying high in the sky made my heart full of happiness while I kissed the sunrise.

Anyway, I looked up to the sky and breathed; I felt my whole entire body was so fresh and the cooling breeze slowly went inside me and I gently blew out – wow, such a joyful morning. I felt my entire sadness flying free from my head and my soul smile, at rest. I was so in love with the beginning of spring and that is one of the reasons I love London: because of the four seasons. For me spring is wonderful and very colourful with glorious happiness, and all the trees bring beautiful flowers with a divine smile that I can't imagine; how beautiful is spring. What make more beautiful on the springtime is the sky is always clear and blue wish I can be on the above together with the morning sky. I stood on the terrace, staring above; I could feel a soft breeze softly blowing my face. So clear, and I could see at the beginning of spring the blue sky smiling at me, and felt like I was flying in heaven to be with my white rose.

My eyes looked at the ground, the grass starting to grow with a light green colour. And I looked at the surrounding leaves starting to come out, which told me that winter had gone. I could feel the breeze, very warm, and the sunlight started to burst everywhere. Again I took a deep breath, thinking day by day I'd struggled with the emotional feeling of writing the story of *Goodbye White Rose*. Rose is natural, and very interesting, but goodbye can be a little emotional. Since I started to write the story of my mum I haven't really been able to sleep during the night; it haunts my dreams. Most of the time I've been in tears with my finger running around with the story. But as I got along with the story I got even stronger, which made me triumph in showing how much I love her.

After forty-five minutes in my garden I decided to spend more time and enjoy the peacefulness of the early morning, the beginning of spring, and listen to my soul and listen to the bird's singing. My favourite bird is the cute robin – the tweet, tweet in the early morning to say good morning to me just puts a smile in my heart. And surprisingly the blackbird is always at the same spot under my pine tree and hopping around as soon as it sees me, maybe to greet me – hey, it is you again. It was phenomenal, especially as I am a bird lover; that's why in the whole year the springtime is the very best season for me. But whatever the season, they're a beauty to behold I'll not to broke for any reason especially mornings are my diamond. All nature, in every season on this planet earth, is magical and breathtaking. That's why every year I can't wait to see nature, especially for spring to arrive, to see the flower open shyly with a smile and the butterflies happily kissing. Every morning in my garden I smell the fresh morning and the natural perfume from many kinds of flowers. Silently my heart whispers and I wish my life would grow each year as glorious as the beautiful season of spring. But nothing I can complain about because I still have such a wonderful life that not many people can have. So I am one of the luckiest people; I thank God for giving me such a wonderful life.

Slowly I take footsteps around my garden and there was a lone white rose sitting at the corner of my garden smiling at me, full of beauty. From afar the smell was so divine, breaking my soul; every time I breathed it took away the pain in my heart. Straight away I stopped at the white rose and looked at the blooming of the white rose, which just reminded me of my mum. The white rose was extraordinarily beautiful and the soft breaths of love were the purest and sweetest thing, exactly like my mum's face. The purest and softest white rose felt like velvet in my heart, when I touched the most perfect roses, just like my mum – the most perfect woman in the world. I stood in the garden of my heart surrounded by lots of greenery, full of flowers, especially the white rose staring at me; it was nurtured by God's own loving care. And my love grew when I saw the white rose, deep-hearted and pure, with scented dew so perfect, which just made me miss my mum deeply. But then I was sad to see it beaten by the wind; I wished my mum was here. To pick the white roses with her would bring me so much happiness.

Gently I stretched my neck to the right and to the left then to the back and closed my eyes with my mind fresh, waking myself up to start the rest of the day. I could feel spring morning winds gently knock my face, then I took a deep breath and slowly opened my eyes; it was sunrise, bright in the whole world. The wind at the beginning of springtime awakes me to see at the sun has smile to me absolutely brilliant. My eyes opened wide and looked at the white rose then continued to enjoy the peaceful morning, full of the natural beauty of earth that I admire. I never want to miss the beauty of the morning, especially hearing the birds singing. It made my broken heart smile. At this point I wanted to be a bird, spread my wings and let the wind take me high to the sky while singing happily all day long until the sunset calls me to settle at night.

Suddenly my imagination was interrupted by a bird singing with a soft voice – it felt magical. There you are – my eyes spot the tiny bluebird on the top of spring flower just on the top of the cherry tree. I was so focused on that tiny bluebird's song but suddenly my mind was interrupted hearing the sound, *zeee... zeee... zeee...* Right in front of me was a bee. I was scared of bees but I was sure he wouldn't sting me if I stayed still. I looked the bee buzzing from one flower to another collecting pollen, surely for making honey. I wished I could be a bee making honey. Definitely I would look ravishing and my face would always glow like a flower – that's all I wanted to be because I love beauty just like my mum. Having many kind of birds flying in front of me singing cheerful songs made me feel free and my soul very cheerful.

Without me expecting it, a white pigeon flew down on the ground and stopped right in front of me which woke my mind up, thinking what message this pigeon had brought for me – obviously not a love letter; there was definitely nothing hanging round the neck. This pigeon, really bravely, walked closer to me with its neck moving like a spring. It just made me smile to see the behaviour – it really gave me a connection to nature. I wished I could talk to this pigeon rather than just stand still like a statue, but my soul whispered, 'Aye up!' The pigeon came close to me. The feather, so white and soft, made me so tempted to stroke it, so I slowly stretched my hand out, wanting to touch the wings. But quickly this pigeon flew away and left me alone without saying goodbye. Well, let me say to the pigeon, 'Bye, lovely pigeon, and have a funny day.' Anyway, my face started to feel a bit warmer and that was because the sun had started to burst and shine everywhere, but the cool from last night was still around. I enjoyed the beginning of a spring morning, full of happiness but still with sadness in my heart, so I decided to have a rest in the summer house.

I was sitting in the summer house in my garden on my own thinking that it had already been two days since my mum left me without a word but goodbye to the world. Even though the morning was so perfect and the skies were blue, from the summer house my eyes couldn't stop looking at the white rose. I felt my mum was still alive. The doves opened their beaks to cry peace and welcome spring

– absolutely glorious, everything coming back to life. From losing my mum just two days ago my heart was still badly broken and my sadness was nowhere near recovering, but I still appreciated what a pure life would bring. Hours passed and I still sat in the summer house with my broken heart. Then slowly I walked out from the summer house and looked at the earth while my mind was thinking my mum all alone inside the earth on the other side of the world. There was a sad feeling but then I listened to the wind blowing while the early spring whispered in my ears, saying, 'Your mum is back where she belongs.' With smile so much pleasure this nature can bring for my new day of spring to be alive on such a morning.

I love spending my time in my garden: feeling the air of spring bringing smells from the earth, blowing in my face, full of beauty, which I needed at this time and with white roses fair like spirit of love felt in my soul. My eyes kept looking at the white rose, so perfectly poised and smiling at me; it just melts my heart. I have a big garden; I create in my garden the beauty of love with red roses in springtime. I can sit for an hour looking at my red roses – they make my soul so peaceful. Red rose reminds me the symbol of friendship than to love example friend than become a lovers. The more I look at my red rose, the more it brings back memories from the beginning of my relationship and that particular person who gave me my fourth red rose for my fourth birthday – so beautiful. And the red rose made my life so happy, full of joy, following the heart of the pure. But the red rose behaviour has chance and bled me slowly in my heart. Without noticing, my cool tears ran down on my cheek while my eyes looked at tiny butterflies above my white rose. I wish I could be a butterfly so I could be above on my white rose all day. Anyhow, every flower on the earth that I've ever seen makes my life glow, like heaven; it just feels like a dream. But in my heart, I feel that life is a gift, it could be a miracle but sometimes can be a total disaster. Well, that is life; nothing much we can do about it. I love that about life because for me life is very challenging and I let life kiss me, play with me and dance with me because this is life and all about life.

The weather is glorious but brings sad thoughts to my mind, thinking about going home to visit my mum's graveyard.

I wanted to walk around in my garden, but the soil was very muddy and dirty, because it rained all night; the April shower started to fall. Last night I hardly slept missing my mum's voice and laugh, but to hear the rain fall was such a beautiful sound and brought tears of joy with each raindrop. Anyway, it made me smile to see the leaves in my garden fresh after the rain last night, especially as my flowers were blossoming. That is why the saying is March winds April showers bring May flowers. The best of all times is a real April day, but all those are thanks to God and Mother Nature for giving us such a stunning life. Before I left my garden suddenly the sun shone bright down on my beautiful garden and the air was cool and clear. Gently I breathed deep into my lungs then tenderly I started to walk and step onto the terrace. Oh dear, the floor was slippery, making me stumble constantly, but luckily I managed to walk right to my kitchen door. With my happy thoughts and letting the sunshine smile at me as well, I left nature alone and let the springtime bring new life because they already make my mornings so marvellous.

Spring Has Sprung

The next day in the early morning I decided to walk in my garden again, but as soon as I opened the kitchen door I could see the wind blowing through the trees and the wind blowing the flowers but brrrrr… the wind was very chilly this morning. Well, the winds kept coming along singing into my ears and kissing me everywhere on my face then they were happily gone. Somehow I'm blessed by the wind for waking me and giving me such a happy smile in the early spring morning. It was April, the cruellest month, and it was very early in the morning so no one was awake yet. The morning was silent and the fog growing thick, which made me hardly able to see anything but I love the fog. I could see a few lampposts on the road and the mist hanging heavy in the air. I then slowly started walking round the circle in my garden but the heavy fog kept slumping into my face; it felt like someone kept giving me wet kisses, which refreshed my morning. My eyes tried to search to see the sky but because the heavy mist and fog were so thick they blocked out my view completely. However, I kept kissing and kissing the mist, and the moist slowly ran into my lungs; it was magnificent. Feeling so magnificent, I thought, 'I can live in this beautiful world forever.'

The next morning, I did the same thing, standing alone in my garden in this beautiful spring, full of sadness deep in my heart because I was unable to see my mum's eyes when she took her last breath. My face was smiling, seeing the spring, when life begins, but my heart was crying because life had taken my mum away. My eyes cried, my heart cried and my soul cried a million times. I cried to know my mum had left me behind and never come back. I couldn't wait to go home to visit my mum's graveyard and to lay her favourite white rose on her grave. And I wished at that time the rain would fall so the rain could soak my roses for her and bloom beautifully.

I know my mum fought so hard to wait for me to come home and I prayed so hard day and night for her because a million times I needed her. If I could save my mum with all the power of magic in God's hand I would but I know she rests in peace in heaven. Losing my mum, I feel a part of me went with her because my connection with her is still fresh, although she's far from me. There's not a moment that I don't think about her; I think about her as soon I open my eyes and I miss her in my dreams. Every night I'll look at the clear sky and when the stars blink my heart whispers words of love with a big smile. Gently I closed my eyes again; with a smile I blew, my breath in the air taken by the winds which would be brought to my mum as well, and that is the secret that I share with nature. All my mum's pictures and videos will be great memories that I will always keep with me forever, but I can't watch them at the moment. I especially can't hear her voice; it would break my heart into a million pieces.

Anyway, yes, spring had sprung and the birds were flying, full of the joy of life. Spring is the beginning of life; after a long sleep the trees start to bring new leaves out and the flowers begin to pop their heads up, nestled in nature's heart. Birth and rebirth are waiting to paint a new landscape to welcome the arrival of spring in an explosion of colours. Spring is fresh and pure, like our innocent childhood, and clean, growing slowly in the hope of a fulfilling and exciting life. Buds emerge everywhere and new leaves of different shades of green cover chestnut trees and the immortal oak trees, and the pick flowers hemming in the chew. Spring would not be spring without birdsong, and spring would be spring without babies crying. Women around the world never stop giving birth every second, minute, day and week, and the same goes for animals. Day after day we can't help growing older but then year after year spring can't help seeming younger. While the wild poppy lights upon the lea and blazes 'Mid the corn' the flowering branches grow naturally some long and some shot exactly likes a human life. The smell of the earth is good, with glorious and natural beauty the daffodils. Every morning is stunning, with the sun bursting out of the sky. It's just happiness to the earth and puts a smile on my face because I know summer is just round the corner; that means we have a longer day. I love to spend time on my own in the morning springtime, to smell the breath of spring and the divine smell of many kinds of flowers on the trees. And I love the mornings of spring; they just make my heart and soul fresh to start my day. My spirit becomes so peaceful, feeling how pure the air of spring is.

Deep down inside me I felt this was the beginning of my life after losing my mum. I always did the same almost every morning and sometimes I just sat quietly, doing nothing, trying to see the grass growing by itself, but I would never be lucky. Spring is a new chapter of life, nature sending everyone messages of rebirth and changes like the light at the end of long and dark journey. Birds building their offspring's nest is a sign of a new chapter in life. And also in time the bird brings their newborn baby to welcome to the world.

It is always happy for me when the season of spring arrives; my heart always feels that this is the best beginning of my life. But now, as I've lost my mum, I will try the best I can to make my life beautiful and colourful like spring on the earth. My wish and hope every day is that the sun will shine on my life. Suddenly I could smell the breath of spring calmly wandering on the air to my soul. I could feel the breeze moving tenderly, crossing through my whole body, then my eyes saw a groups of birds singing beautifully – it makes life so exciting. To hear and see the nature of beauty is what I wait for every year in the springtime. It was so fun to see the cheeky squirrels chasing each other, fighting for the nuts, and running up and down from the trees, putting a smile in my heart. And a little adorable red robin hopping around, happily playing in the springtime; it made me want to hold it in my hand. While I kept all my sadness in one corner of my heart, my life was getting so great in this moment that I just wanted to see the rainbow to make more wishes. And to see the beautiful colours of the rainbow, which just makes my life even more glorious in the new time of spring. The sunshine made all the trees in my garden very shining, clear and colourful. I was going to be full of joy in this beautiful spring, and to be able to see the rebirth of Mother Nature is sensational.

Animal born bring babies in spring with the beautiful weather and the food to prepare them for adulthood in good conditions. Especially the birds; as soon as the newborn have arrived they will tweet! tweet! happily. I can see between the green leaves that many nests have been built by lots of birds. Their best chance of surviving will be if they are strong and independent enough for the rainy and cold season. When spring starts to burst into the world human faces are very cheerful and the animals wake from hibernation; this is how God creates the beauty of life. How amazing that when springtime arrives nature keeps bringing happiness to the earth and making the world smile. As every morning in springtime I love to look at the white rose in my garden so I opened my window and looked at it.

Anyhow, after my delicious meal I decided to step out the darkest night for a walk around to settle my food down. As my house has a beautiful garden I was very happy to just walk around between all my plants blown by the night winds. I silently stood under the huge pine tree; suddenly my eyes spotted a few insects flying in the darkness. But all those insects made my body not move anywhere because I am scared of insects. All the birds and squirrels returned to their trees to rest for the night. I looked at the sky; it was calm and misty but I could hear the sound of the evening winds, so soft and tender. And so I did not wake all those birds that could be sleeping on the pine tree I gently took my feet and moved from there to let them have a peaceful night. I was on my own sitting in the garden with the beautiful night bringing me so much joy and peace to my soul. Once again I could hear the wind singing in my ears and smiled as it blew past my face – wow! Life is so pure. I decided to spend more time in the garden looking at the clear sky and counting the stars in heaven while the full moon overlooked me. Ummm… luckily enough the full moon coming made my night even more glorious. Thank you, full moon, you have done a spiffing job for me. I then looked at the trees moving tenderly blown by the night wind then heard the breeze; it was so calm. All of a sudden I heard the crickets screaming, calling their friends to sleep. From my garden I could see people walking with bags or a briefcase in hand rushing back home from work. As the night had just begun many cars in the streets passed by while the early spring night winds brought life followed by the secret of love. I thought that at the beginning of spring I have to learn a lot about the beauty of nature as every year I always look forward to springtime. Slowly I circled my neck around and looked up at the sky, the clouds slowly moving, turning to grey. Gently I took a breath and smelt the earth from the beginning of springtime; it just made me want to stay all night long to see how the nature would change during the night. And I looked at the earth but then the world started to go silent; it was the time that the true magical midnight of spring had begun. Such a marvellous evening, so it was time for me to go inside and to hit the sack.

The month of April brings so much life; because of that I love to go out and enjoy that the springtime has arrived. Especially to hear the birds sing – absolutely beautiful, making my day happy while the spring winds kiss everywhere. So one morning I decided to go Kew Gardens to enjoy the nature of spring and take my mind away from thinking about my mum for a few hours, which give me so much sadness. Honestly this was the second time I'd gone down to Kew gardens, even though I'd been living in United Kingdom for about thirty years now. Anyway, Kew Gardens is a world-famous botanical garden and it took me about thirty minutes by car from where I live. It was in the spring of 2022. I entered Kew Gardens, where many people were walking around and as lovers holding hands romantically. The atmosphere surrounding Kew Gardens was breathtaking, especially with the rare flowers that I'd never seen before.

I freed myself for a day walking around Kew Gardens and listening to many kinds of birds singing. Suddenly I spotted the bluebirds, which happens to me every time April showers come along. Straight away I stood quietly for a few moments listening to the whistles and chirps become beautiful melodies which create a secret song from bluebirds. I wanted to continue my walk but the bluebirds looked at me and sang even louder, which just made me smile in my heart. Soon the bluebirds stopped singing; I slowly left them and let them gossip with each other.

I then continued my walk in Kew Gardens to see many kind of flowers, and there were cockleshells, tulips red and green, daffodils and Chinese quill. All those flowers are beautiful colour which brightest my life ever seen especially the bluebells wake on summers down. Actually I'd never heard and never seen the bluebells before until this moment standing right in front of the bluebells. But before I came to Kew Gardens one of my friends told me about the bluebells and he was so crazy about seeing the bluebells. At that time I wondered what was so special about the bluebells, which make me so curious to know more about the bluebells. But before I went to Kew Gardens I read and found out about the bluebells which made it easier for me to understand. Now to see the bluebells beautifully laid out like a giant carpet filling the forest floor – honestly at that moment I was falling in love with bluebells. Surprisingly it just took me a few minutes to see the bluebells and now the bluebells are my favourite flower. As far as I know bluebells are an English plant and grow only in the United Kingdom. What is so special about bluebells is that they arrive every time April showers coming along, meaning they are a British sign of spring. When I looked at the bluebells I felt like I was in a secret garden of love; it was so romantic, like God's sweet love. In late spring bluebells often grow so close together they transform the woodland floor into a dazzling carpet of shimmering blue. When I looked at every wild bluebells' little flowers they made my softened heart feel blissful in ways that words could never describe.

I was very lucky that the weather was very bright; it was a sunny day and the sun burst on a single sweet bluebell. That day my heart and soul were free to spend a thankful life. Slowly I took my feet and left the bluebells' secret garden of love and walked carelessly along the sunny lane where oak and beech and hazel trees stood. Not far from me I saw a beautiful cottage which I went around and stood and stood while my mind was miles away; it reminded me of my childhood. It put a smile in my heart, and the cries of birds made me lost for words. I then continued walking around the woodland, enjoying the colours of many kinds of flowers and leaves while the afternoon sun shone on me. I thought, 'Should I go soon or should I stay more?', but my feet started to get tired. At the same time I could hear the birds singing loud, maybe trying to say goodbye to me, so I knew now was the time for me to go.

Without noticing I'd walked quite far and miles away to find the way out. But I did not rush to go anywhere, just took my time and enjoyed being surrounded by natural beauty in the month of April. Because every season would arrive just once a year so I should make the most of it. Out of the blue my eyes spotted a sign in the wood with the word woodpecker. I was so excited, wanting to see the woodpecker so much. I wanted, I wished and I prayed that I would see woodpecker before I left this place. It reminded me of when I was teenager; I always watched the cartoon of Woody Woodpecker with my mum and my mum loved it, so to see a woodpecker in the flesh would be a dream come true. If I saw the woodpecker today it would be a miracle. For almost ten minute I wandered around but there was no sign of the woodpecker. I thought, 'I'll give it another ten minutes.' Voila! My heart jumped high as soon as I soon as I heard the sound from the wood: peck, peck, peck, peck… peck… I knew this was coming from the woodpecker. Quickly my eyes opened wide to find the woodpecker while my ear tried to follow the sound. It was so funny; my eyes opened wide and didn't blink. Within a few minutes I saw a tiny bird, so sweet, very pretty with a long beak. He poked out his head and he had on a hood with collar of red. My heart screamed, 'Oh my goodness! That is a woodpecker. *Wow!* This is absolutely amazing.' I would never forget my time seeing the woodpecker today. I tried to walk closer to the tree where he was knocking to make his nest. I let my heart fill with so much love for him.

Silently I sat under the tree while my eyes saw the clouds moving in the sky; it made me feel in my soul so much love towards him. I looked at him, never missing a single tap that he did until my mind reached the sky, whispering, 'Come, little woodpecker, fly to me so I can tell you that I am in love with you.' The day was calm, a bright sunny day, which made me want to knock on his door. But I am not young enough anymore to climb up the tree and disturb their house like I used to do when I was a young girl. Anyhow, I could see his eyes reaching out to the ground looking down at me where I sat. Straight away I gave him a big smile while I dreamt all about him; suddenly he flew away and left me behind on my own. My heart wanted to scream, to say, 'Please don't go,' but I was sure he was scared. But I had a brilliant moment with the woodpecker knocking and the day floating by in April.

Anyhow, I started to feel hungry and butterflies started to make sounds in my stomach. So I decided to find the café; after a ten-minute walk I could see a few cafés where I could choose to have lunch. I could see a lot of people sitting outside exposing their body to the sun trying to get their body tanned – well, of course that was not me. Here I was, standing outside, and I chose 'Pick 'n' Mix Café'. There were a few empty seats inside but with the pandemic of course I decided to sit outside, obviously under an umbrella as the sun would not get to my skin. But then I had to go inside to choose what I wanted as no menus were handed to me – that meant self-service. OK, soon I entered inside; straight away I could see there were sandwiches, which were not my cup of tea, but they had many kinds of chocolate cakes which I love very much. Sadly I was trying to control my weight at that moment. Even though my eyes and my mouth were drooling looking at it, I had to be straight. At the end I decided to have a seafood salad which would be good for me to lose some of my weight. I was on my own with a delicious seafood salad mixed with parmesan cheese, which is my not favourite, black olives and olive oil, which I love very much, and the taste of fresh lemon juice – so refreshing in this springtime. I had enjoyed my own company and enjoyed looking at beautiful view, dark and blue. Funnily enough I couldn't even remember what day it was, but it was sunny and sometimes turned chilly. The world moves but because of gravity we don't feel it – how cool is nature? I breathed the fresh air deeply and freed my mind from the stress and I felt that my soul seemed to reach heaven. I felt my life was so peaceful, which put a smile on my face – gosh! I smiled on my own quickly and turned my head, pretending to look around in case someone thought I was crazy. I don't think anyone noticed me because there were busy laying in the sun with their eyes closed. I was feeling a little hot so I opened my topknot and let the wind play with my hair. The air of spring brought smells from the earth to my face, full of beauty, which I needed.

After an hour sitting enjoy my seafood salad it was now time for me to kick my ass out of this café to continue my visit to Kew Gardens. Out of the blue my feet wanted to touch and kiss the earth so I decided to walk barefoot on the grass. The tiny white flowers between my feet felt even more comfortable. As I walked past the woods my eyes saw some blurred little creature with a furry curly tail hop up to the tree and run down to the ground – it was a squirrel. Luckily I had some seeds and nuts in my bag so I grabbed a few nuts and gently handed them to the little squirrel. He looked at me with friendly eyes but then snapped the nut out of my hand, quickly put it in his jaws and ran up to the tree. I looked at him and smiled and I thought he was rather sweet. Gently I took a sip of fresh air and walked away from that cute squirrel while looking at all the trees covered up with leaves. To listen to the birds singing happily on the cherished earth I thought this world was full of life. I am very blessed to stay in this rich beautiful earth of England which gives me roses to love in life. Every time I thought about it, it took my breath away, flying in the air, and my heart was at peace in heaven. I looked around, the sun still bursting everywhere, but sometimes a cloud came over, which made me worried about the April showers. The wind was still but sometime came and made my body a bit chilly. Luckily I had my jumper with me. Without me noticing, I had been walking in Kew Gardens for two hours since I arrived at midday when the sun started to burst.

Anyway, I had a glorious day clearing up my brain and I felt my life was splendid, seeing the beauty of nature. Honestly, the natural beauty on this earth makes people's lives so perfect. But before I left Kew Gardens I knew I would love to go in the greenhouse to see tropical plants with exotic, colourful flowers. Without wasting time I quickly entered the greenhouse and the first thing that hit me was the climate and rainforest; it just reminded me of being back home Malaysia. I enjoyed looking at every single plant, especially the hibiscus rosa, sinensis, or in my language it is bunga raya. Hibiscus is the national flower of Malaysia and of course the state flower of Hawaii. I believe it is known as the queen of tropical flowers, as it is said to signify peace and bravery. It reminded me of when I was a little girl staying in the countryside. I love hibiscus flowers and I think they are full of beauty with bright colours. They had them in white, pink and a few more colours, but my favourite is red. Every day I would pick one red hibiscus flower and put it in between my ear, and I thought I looked so pretty. These days I sometimes put hibiscus flower in my topknots but of course they are artificial and still look pretty.

On my way out from the greenhouse I saw a banana plant which again reminded me of my childhood. My father planted lots of banana trees round the house so we never bought bananas. As I come from a poor family bananas did a lot for our daily basics. My mum was a very good cook and she created many kind of dishes with bananas. As far as I remember with the green bananas my mum would make curry with dried salted fish; obviously she never forgot coconut milk and we ate it with rice. It was delicious to eat in the afternoon but nowadays as I am very careful with my cholesterol I won't eat curry anymore. Not for bananas but because of coconut milk: I hate coconut milk. Well, not just bananas; my mother could make dishes with even bananas' blossoms. My mum would cook bananas' blossoms with prawns or dried anchovies, again with coconut milk, of course, and that was another delicious dish created by my mum. And I remember every morning my mum would cut the bananas into slices and dip them into flour which was already mixed with water then put them into hot oil. She left the bananas in the wok until the colour of the flour turned gold brown. My mother would serve it hot so myself and my brothers picked it up quickly and bit every single slice of banana – mmm… so yummy, crunchy and sweet. That was in the countryside before but nowadays it is most popular eaten as a snack or at tea time. What surprises me is that they even have fried bananas in restaurants in London as a dessert. Well, the banana dish that I love the most is banana pancake – the truth is that I even learned from my mum how to make it. This dish is a traditional dishes which was my favourite childhood breakfast growing up. Banana pancakes will always be my favourite, especially as bananas are very good and nutritious. And the last thing is the banana leaf; my mum always cooked coconut rice but my mum wrapped coconut rice inside the banana leaf and the coconut rice would smell absolutely divine. I could eat and eat without stopping. My mum was a very good cook and she could do a lot of things and create her own dishes – she was amazing at a lot of things. Anyway, there was not a lot different comparing that with Indian food; they eat rice on the plate but they eat on the banana leaf. It was very different but very tasty too.

Well, I guessed it was time for me to go home and leave all the natural beauty in peace – I wished I could stay a little longer but time wouldn't allow me to do so. However I was so glad I'd made the decision to come to Kew Gardens; I felt like all the evil had gone away from my sight. It was like a daydream, of a happy time. On my way out my eyes looked at all the trees with flowers moving left and right like they were waving at me. And my ears heard many kinds of bird screaming, saying goodbye; it was a spectacular day which put a huge smile on my face and my heart. However, April showers made my day full of sunlight, and introduced me to natural beauty, some of which I'd never known before. Anyway, as soon as I was out from the gate of Kew Gardens my legs started to feel tired from three hours' walking and again it took me more or less fifteen minutes by foot to get to the train station. Next to the station there was a café and there were a few tables outside with beautiful people sitting enjoying drinks with company. But one table under the tree was empty; I thought it would be nice to sit and rest my feet. Without wasting time I ran and got the table before someone else could have it. Gosh, I can't explain how relieved I was to sit and to let my feet out my shoes. I already had a my knee problem and now my feet were really killing me. A long time ago I used to teach aerobics for three, four hours a day and dance all night long in the club and my feet were still smiling full of energy until the next day and the rest of the day. But now this was all gone as I'd grown older; every part of the body became like they were secondhand. Well, that is life.

Anyhow, I could see many people walking towards the station; surely all those people were coming from Kew Gardens. I though my whole body had recharged then, although my feet were not ready to go inside my shoes, but they had to, especially as the sun had started to lower, which give me a warning that I had to make a move. I could hear that the next train would arrive in a few minutes so I rushed to the platform before I missed it. While I was in the train my mind was wondering about nature and life, and that they are similar concepts because nature is the study of how life acts and interacts within the circle of existence. Inside the train I looked at the view outside and the world smiled at me and light brilliant trees freshly brushed. The sky was still blue and the bright sun burst on my face, making me so tired and my eyes drowsy, wanting to sleep.

In the lovely evening I lay on my sofa after a long day for my feet, doing the walking. The evening was cool but I could see from my window that the sunset was glorious, giving me so much joy in sorrow. Every time it took my breath away; I felt my heart was beyond the world. The evening air made my mind think about the food that meant it was time for dinner, especially as my body had used all my energy today. With my sore feet I gently took a step towards the kitchen to see what I could have for dinner. I felt my knee was too weak to stand in the kitchen making my dinner so I grabbed a packet of fast noodles – it just took me a few minutes to prepare them, which made my life so much easier. And it was also fast to eat – it just took me about fifteen minutes to finish my fast noodles, which gave me plenty of time to enjoy my evening and go to bed early.

After dinner I went into my bedroom and my eyes looked at my silky nightgown. I think the month of April is nice to feel silk on my body so I grabbed my silk nightgown and slowly it put on, which then smoothly touched all my skin and stroked every inch of my body as soon as I walked. I felt silk tenderly kissing my skin, which make me so in love with silk.

I wandered into the living room with a glass of red wine. I not a drinker and I don't drink alcohol but people say a glass of red wine is good for your heart, and it also can help me to unwind from a stressful day. A single sip or two makes me feel a little woozy and makes me forget about depressing things in life. As my body started to feel tingly it made me laugh a little but my soul travelling to hundreds mile spell of heart of lover. At that moment the red wine made me think it would be wonderful to have some company. Also the red wine made my body hot so I opened the window to get some fresh air at midnight.

Straight away my eyes spotted the full moon in the sky looking down at me on the earth with a smile. I thought, 'What a beautiful night it is when the sun settles down.' With the wine glass still in my hand I looked up at the skies and closed my eyes sharing my moment, wishing I had someone with me to share this beautiful night. But hey! It's not the end of the world; I still enjoyed it on my own with the glowing moon and happy stars which just made my night splendid. Especially in this silent breeze; I just wished an angel would come down from heaven then it would be the most perfect night ever. My heart was restless which meant my night had settled down.

When I wanted to close the door suddenly I felt drops of rain on my hand. That reminded me of my mum; she hated rain because it gave her a headache when the rain touched her head. But I loved to see rain drop heavily like cats and dogs; it is magical to think how the water can drop from the sky and the sky can hold mountains of water. To look at the rain reminds me of my mum; when she was a little girl growing up in the countryside it always rained heavily. When the rain stopped and a rainbow came out then my mum thought the rainbow would create magnificent life. So my mum always waited for the rain to settle because sometimes if she was lucky she would see the rainbow. Some people love rain and they will walk, run, dance and sing in the rain – well, not my mum. As soon as I used to see the rainbow burst from the skies, my mum would dance and sing under the rainbow with so much happiness. My mum loved the rainbow because it made her think life was sometimes full of colours like a rainbow. And rainbows made my mum cheerful when I think about my difficult childhood. But it was very funny for myself; when I was a little girl I thought the rainbow was a snake with seven colours coming from heaven to drink water from earth. Because of that I always wanted to see which side was the head and which side was the tail, it but never happened and that was the reason I always looked forward to seeing the rainbow. Before the rainbow disappeared I always made a wish; even today when I see a rainbow I still make a wish.

Well, sadly tonight I couldn't see the rainbow as rainbows never come during the night. Anyway, rain started to drop heavily; I let the rain kiss my lips before I shut the window then I jumped straight in my bed, covered my body with a warm blanket and surrounded myself with a few extra pillows and small cushions. My mind slowly disappeared listening to the rain dancing around on the roof, lost in the midnight April shower.

The Summer Chapter of Life

It was a summer day and the morning sun glowed; it looked like it was going to be a sunny day. I was looking forward to it but then after thirty minutes suddenly the sky was covered in a blanket of clouds. No wonder I felt so warm last night; obviously the heat from last night was going to produce rain this morning in the summer month of June. Gently I stuck out my head out the window; the wind blew so freshly but sadly the skies were darkening. Within a few minutes the thunder shocked me with a big noise from above; it really freaked me out. And within a second lightning flashed across my kitchen – wow, I almost shit my pants. I ran to the living room with my hot green tea listening to the thunder and lightning crash on a summer morning. From my window I could see the rain pouring heavily; it was beautiful to see the rain mix with the sun. But it lasted only fifteen minutes; then the rain softly dropped and began to stop and the summer sky turned blue; everywhere was magical. I had a huge smile when I heard the birds calling their mates to play again – it meant the weather was going to be good all day. Thank

God the rain didn't last long and the sun was bursting everywhere again – gosh, this summer thunderstorm was amazing. And now it had become one bright summer – life would bring me so much joy for the rest of my day and in the days to come. Summer in London lasts for three months if you're lucky so we took advantage, having fun, because the day seemed to last forever and the fun never stopped. The sun could be very strong during summer time but it is the time of romance and enjoying life. To create the family and career plain that feeling of eternal life need and belong.

I am a morning person especially in the summer mornings; I wake up before the sun wakes me. From Monday to Friday I will spend my time in my garden when the air is still cool to cleanse my soul of any issues and enjoy looking at nature and the tree preparing themselves. Sometimes I stand in the middle of my garden and my mind thinks that I deserved a rest, reflecting on my past and future. Surrounding me, nature peacefully prepares for mornings in summer. What I love about in my garden is my stupendous pine tree with many kinds of birds on it. The prelude of annuity bit me and kept walking hoping to hold on to third magical moment. But on Saturday and Sunday I love to stay in bed all morning, put my blanket to one side and let my body feel fresh and breathe. Then I keep my mind together while my eyes slightly admire things, going into a daydream with a smile on my face. How beautiful the mornings are when summer days are long.

Anyway, I stood by the window looking at the busy road full of smoke and the noisy city of London, but I could feel the air close with heat. The heat made me very thirsty so I went to the kitchen and grabbed my glass, added some ice and poured pure coconut juice. I've never liked ice and I haven't had ice for yonks, but because of the heat I fancied having a little ice. Anyhow, I brought the coconut juice to the living room and let it rest on the table before I drank it. I took myself close to the window and viewed the garden. Wow, absolutely brilliant – I could see the tulips, very fresh and clean, but bees kissed the tulip over and over; so beautiful. My white rose was striking, the white colour sweet and romantic while the butterflies were kissing the white rose so gently and the sun shone brightly for most of the day. Suddenly I felt sweat slowly run over my body and my throat was getting so dry. I grabbed my coconut drink and took a gentle sip – mmm… the cool and the sweet feeling of fresh coconut touching my lips. Oh… my goodness, it was a sensational feeling in the summer afternoon. I love the summer but I don't like the sun, especially as I'm not very good with the heat. Again from my window I could see the sun was shining and life was very precious so I didn't want to waste a single minute doing nothing. My mind tried to make a plan to do things on the hot, gorgeous summer day, especially as today was the hottest day. Not tomorrow, because tomorrow is another day and another day to enjoy, but today was a beautiful day. My brain was jumping high, seeing the sun shining everywhere; it made my life and spirit alive again. Somehow summer never seemed to last long enough, so I would take the opportunity while the sun was full of a smile and make the most of it before it went.

On this bright summer day I was on the road walking to the high street happily, my life full of joy, but wow, it was extremely hot. As much as I love the summer, I can't stand the sun; straight away I felt my face being hit by the heat. While I was walking I could feel the humidity burning the earth as much as it was burning myself. Well, in London summer time only lasts for three months or maybe less, so I would try every day to make myself as bright as summer. The happiness made me smile on my own and I danced a little while walking; it felt like a magical dream for me. Also the summer day made the world very bright, colourful and magical; it lit up the skies – so very mystical.

This bright day too reminded me about my mum; the humidity made my mum sit outside under the tree, enjoying the afternoon winds. At one stage my mum told me that she wished someone would enter her life and show her the way to heaven, sleeping on a gold bed with dreams of love and be pampered like a princess. At that time my mum had a broken heart with my dad especially treating her really bad. And my mum felt his love like piercing pain after he broke her heart into pieces. My mum then continued her life with so much pain but hiding all soreness and kept smiling so her eyes never rained. This was the worst thing to ever happen in my mum's love life but he fled and enjoyed his next delusion in life. He left my mum on her own with so much loneliness and at that time my mum often sat under the leafless lonely tree;' it just made her feels better. Without noticing, tears ran down on my cheeks. I then quickly wiped them away before someone noticed it. From there my mum made life full of magic and kept herself strong and steady with her feet firmly on the ground. And she secretly searched in the dark for the missing pieces of her broken heart and made it her real life with pure love. And here I am with my own bright life as a strong woman, like my mother. Gently I looked up at the blue sky showing this beautiful world; it made me think that I only have one life. I looked around the park; the sunshine all around brought my happiest, brightest summer life. Summertime is too hot. The eye of heaven shone again, reminding me of when I was just a little girl playing around. I felt time's gentle, loving touch but did not think of it too much as a road that ends beyond the sun and I didn't know when summer ended.

Anyway, I was still in the high street looking at the people. Dear lord, I felt like I was somewhere seeing a concert. That is London: as soon as the sun is out they go crazy, rushing out, having fun and lying in the sun, trying to get their body tanned. Obviously not me; I am very different from them. I'm scared of the sun and will try to escape and cover my skin as much as I can so it does not get dark. But I still was having fun sitting in the café looking at the people walking past and enjoying a jar of Pimms on the table with blooming flowers, juicy fruits, blueberries and rock melons while the children were enjoying licking an ice cream. I also could feel the youth and the new taste of freedom, the discoveries, the mistakes and the adventures, the enjoyment and the first pain of losing my mum. The sunshine was still full everywhere and many men opened their tops, walking around with their dogs, showing off their healthy tan. And not far from me was a little park and I can see many women lay on the grass with the naked tan and bikini line cry for stares on the summer afternoon just make the parks alive. To see all those crowded pf peoples have always been in my heart with two most beautiful words in English expression which is, summer makes a silence after spring and birds singing summer song.

I sat in the café for thirty minutes, but the sun was so strong against my skin I was almost going to melt – I wished I was sitting indoors. Anyway, my stomach was full of food and my body started to get a little tired. But the day was still a long way from night so I had plenty of time to spend in the café. My eyes looked up at the blue sky with the sun in my heart while my ears were listening to wild birds singing happily; it reminded me of when I was with my mum in the jungle in Malaysia. But thank God, who's watching from heaven, because he didn't make my mum suffer for too long. For three days all of us had a very difficult time, seeing my mum's last breaths, her being taking away from this planet earth. I was praying hard for her not to suffer; if it was time for my mum to go, please take her peacefully. It was an absolute miracle that God listened to my prayers and God loves her more than I do. My mum didn't suffer long – *thank God* from my heart for taking my mum safely to heaven. This was very magnificent blessing from God.

I didn't know how long I would be sitting in the café but I could sit all day appreciating the beauty of nature's glory while my mind flew away, thinking and giving me strength within my soul. I could feel the wind flowing across to my face and my eyes looked at the birds flying high, surely to settle their life's journey for a day. I wanted to continue thinking of the journey of my life with my mum but my thoughts would never end. Again the winds blew across my face for the second time; it awakened my soul, then when I looked, the summer afternoon was settling down after a hot day. It was time for me to make a move. Within a minute I left the café while the sky was still clear but with so much sadness and my heart thinking, 'My mum deserved to be in this world for longer with loving and protection.'

Anyway, the evening was a warm summer's day so I decided to relax in my garden and have a light dinner alone. My favourite salad is wild Alaskan salmon with Sicilian cherry tomato and a glass of Pimms – very refreshing. I was sitting in my garden, where the chair and table were already prepared for me, having an early dinner and trying to make my soul peaceful. My eyes lifted to see the silent sky and the beauty of the summer day made my soul dance in my garden. Gently I took a sip of Pimms, which ran slowly down my throat – so divine – while watching the robins, ready jump into their nests. And I removed my shoes, put my both feet on the ground while my toes poked out. Suddenly my ear heard the voice of bees buzzing around my salad – wooops! Quickly I chased the bees away from my salad. Poor things – sorry, little bees, my salad didn't have any pollen to make honey. Without wasting more time I started to eat my salmon salad before the bees returned again. My favourite dish – it reminds my body to keep slim, especially in summertime, otherwise my summer dress won't fit me. I did sprinkle some balsamic vinegar and extra virgin olive oil in my salad – mmm... yummy! Wild Alaskan salmon, my favourite fish in the whole world; the meat was very tender. As soon I bite it, it melted away into my belly. And the Sicilian cherry tomato was rich with a red colour and crunchy when I bit it and the taste was so sweet; it was just the perfect dish for the summer evening. After finishing my pretty meal I decided to spend the evening in my garden and let the wind blow on my warm face with the breeze feeling so cool and refreshing. Suddenly the tiny dragonfly swung in front of me but I couldn't hear any noise. The flowers around my garden were filled with natural perfume. Not long after the summer evening seemed to say to me that the daylight was done, so it was time for me to get out from the garden, but I had such a marvellous time spending the evening on my own with my mum's soul in my heart.

It was at nine in the evening. As I can't sit around doing nothing my feet were asking me to go out for walk which I agreed to. Before going out I switched on the television but I made sure to switch off the lights so I didn't use more electricity which would go on my bill. I walked through the alleyway, my ears suddenly hearing grasshoppers scratching in the bush and all the birds sitting in their nest silently. I decided to sit around and enjoy the sweet summer night while feeling the wind softly swing my green silk dress, which tenderly rubbed my skin – absolutely superb. Then I grabbed my ponytail and removed the rubber band, letting my long black hair flow and dance while my eyes opened wide, watching the happy sky. The air was soft and peaceful, making my mind fly high in the sky, then suddenly my whole body shook to see a huge rat running across and disappearing under a bunch of dry leaves. To see the rat was like seeing the devil; I am very scared of rats – really they are my nightmare. But the lonely night calmed my heartbeat down and I could hear the gentle voice of my soul whispering that the night belongs to the world. That meant it was time for me to let the beauty of nature be on its own. On my way home I could see the moon moving slowly but then it was lost behind a cloud; also a few stars twinkled, just making my night full of joy.

Here I was sitting in my room in the summer at midnight while the breeze blew through my open window. My eyes looked at the silent midnight view and my ears heard the owls calling; it made my blood run, scared to be in my body. I am a bird lover but not for owls. Owls' faces scare me; in fact in Malaysia people call them ghost birds. Oh, bugger, all my hair was standing up as soon as I thought about owls, especially when I saw the moon happily smile and heard the dog start to bark. I felt the midnight spirit voice walk towards the window and without wasting time I rushed to shut the window before whoever it was entered my room. I tried so hard to sleep but my eyes took time to be tired; this was because my mind was thinking about my mum too much. At that moment my life was full to the top and I was very happy that I would be going home soon to visit my mum's graveyard, but at the same time it put me under so much pressure in my chest and made me stressed. However, I prayed hard day and night, hoping everything would be fine so I could go home safely to my mum's graveyard. My happy tears warmly ran down my cheek as I had with smile on my face thinking about my relationship with my mum. My mum's life and mine are similar: struggling at the beginning and we both went through everything in life but we survived. And now my new life without my mum would start soon and that kept my spirit lifted.

Slowly I got up from my the bed, walked towards the window and slowly stretched my neck to look up at the sky; all I could see was the full moon at its brightest. With a smile in my heart I whispered, 'Goodnight, moon.' I could see the stars surrounding the moon blinking at me. With my soft voice I said, 'Goodnight, stars, it's time for me to go sleep now.' And lastly I looked at the world covered with the silence of midnight, making my blood draw inside me. Quickly I shut the window and left the natural beauty in peace then went straight to my silky bed. Since my eyes were getting so tired, straight away I tucked myself in and everything melted away. 'Goodnight, Mum, and goodnight to the world.'

Age of Life in Autumn

Autumn is not my favourite season but I love it just because it takes place around September 21 or 22, and my birthday is September 23. So the beginning of autumn reminds everyone of my birthday, but in Malaysia September is in the rainy season. I started to feel sad when the season of autumn arrived because the leaves would start to change colour and my mum had gone. However before the green leaves say goodbye to the tree, they change colour to red to yellow and brown, then the leaves start to fall off from the tree. Leaves lie on the ground like a golden carpet and fall on the roof, jumping and dancing when the wind comes along. Soon the leaves are completely gone from the trees then the trees look like they've gone for long time. Very sad, but this is God's natural creation. And the birds fly away, moving from one place to another for a long time. In Malaysia people do have the season of autumn; it is called fall. Many leaves from trees fall, especially leaves from the rubber trees. When rubber trees' leaves fall people have to stop doing rubber tapping because the tree can't produce the milk; luckily fall only lasts for two months.

Funnily enough the temperatures never change: hot and humid compared to London, where the weather starts to get cooler when autumn arrives. So we start to wear long-sleeved shirts, long pants and sweaters; the warmth of the sunshine summer is gone, only the whispering breeze stays around.

It was at the end of September and the weather was getting cool; the wind from the north was bringing rain. My eyes looked up at the sky, a bunch of grey clouds cuddling up together, which made the autumn sun hide behind the cloud. It made me so lazy, not wanting to step out, so I decided to keep myself nice and cosy indoors. Sitting on my lonely antique peacock chair by the window, I enjoyed the autumn day while watching the flowers drooping. It was absolutely beautiful to see the leaves fall on the ground one after another and the sky seemed to wave at me; it made me feel like there are miracles in life. Suddenly I can feel the moment to fresher beauty in my soul is rise and fly without wing. From my window I could see showers sprinkle softly down and the sun was out to welcome the autumn day; it made me begin to smile. I kept myself calm, not too over-excited, so with a peaceful mind I decided to go for a walk on the high street. Sadly I had to keep all my summer outfits in my cupboard and summer shoes back in a shoe rack. So I had no choice but to wear my tracksuit, close a hood around my head, wear my trainers and sunglasses – just perfect for walk on the first day of autumn.

Again walking through the alleyway I could see beautiful golden and rusty leaves covering the ground but was so sad to see the trees naked. On my way to the high street there is a little park which I entered and straight away I felt the new beginning of autumn air – so freshening. All the grass had turned brown and grey and was lying flat on the ground, and the park was silent without birdsong. The autumn morning had a shining sun but was quite a chilly morning. I decided to walk round the little lake while watching some wild ducks fly then land in the lake. My legs had less energy to walk around the park so I decided to sit on the bench under the trees right in front of the lake. The breeze brushed my cheeks, turning my face rosy; at the same time I gave a kiss to the clean breeze. I removed the hood and let the wild wind blow my long black hair while my whole body enjoyed the silent morning and autumn air. My heart softly whispered that surely winds from heaven would bring an angel to sing a secret song to me. This mild autumnal morning made my tender heart grow fresher; I wanted to meet a great angel from heaven to tell me all about my mum. My eyes watched the lonely trees against the morning sun and my mind was a mile away, enjoying the nature, just hoping a miracle would happen. Suddenly my blood stopped; I could feel something touching my head. Gently I rubbed my long hair and grabbed a golden leaf stuck in my hair. Stretching my neck up I could see leaves falling from the trees into my long black hair. It put a smile on my face; I wished an angel from heaven would touch my head and give me some magical life from my mum.

Anyway, my body started to feel cool, brrr... So to help me lessen the chill of the windy autumn I continued my walk to the high street to grab a cup of my favourite hot drink, which is hot cocoa. There I was in the café slowly sipping my thick hot cocoa with chocolate powder and the sweetness sticking to my lips. I left it to dry and gently licked my lips; it was so delightful and I tried to make it last. The hot cocoa made my spirit lift; the more I sipped, the more I felt my soul become warmer. With my saddened heart I stood outside the café thinking that summer had already been blow away and left the leafless trees bare in the autumn. Anyway, the sun had started to shine so it was time for me to make a move back home; it was glorious morning I'd had in autumn, which I'd enjoyed with my spirit.

Time is precious for me so I will never let time go by for nothing. Every day I have something to do and every single second, minute and hour I chase the time before the day ends. The same with every season; I never waste any season without appreciating and enjoying the natural beauty given by God. The good thing about natural beauty is that they stay beautiful forever; even the trees can sleep for six months and wake up again. But the difference for humans is that the child turns into an adult, the young becomes old and when it is time we will die and be forever gone from the planet full of natural beauty. And this happened to my mum; it was time for her to go and she went forever from this planet earth and would never come back. Sometimes I am scared of getting old and scared to die; it makes me very sad when I think about it. But this is life; everyone has got to go one day, not just me. Nowadays people's lives can be very short, so everything in life and the seasons that we receive – just enjoy and make the most of them. Stop moaning, just thank God that he gave us more life to live on this planet.

I was spending the chilly autumn looking out of my window; I could see an afternoon wind blowing the leaves that had fallen on the ground. I could see the milky sky, though it was very moody, which made my heart dance as I accepted that the beauty of nature starts with the journey. At that peaceful moment suddenly I saw above my window a butterfly dancing happily in the air and the sky clear everywhere. Silently I stood by the window and watched the butterfly and closed my eyes with a smile; it reminded me of when I was a little girl: my mum always told me that when the butterfly entered the house it meant that someone had come to propose to you –I love my mum's words. So I stood still, trying not to move, just looking at butterfly thinking that maybe this butterfly was sending a message and bringing good news for me. Without wasting any more time I opened the window wide so the butterfly could come in. Quickly I went to sit in the chair looking at the window and praying that that butterfly would enter the house. Within a few seconds the butterfly cheerfully flew inside the house and landed on my table right in front of me. Wow! I thought, 'This is magical, you are very special and welcome to have a date with me.' I rushed to the window and quickly closed it before the butterfly could fly out, then I returned to my seat. The wings had such brilliant bright blue colours; I guessed it could be a male butterfly. It looked very pretty and this was the perfect time for me to make a wish. As soon as I finished my sweet moment with the butterfly it started to fly in a circle round the house. One minute it landed on the wall and the next minute it flew nervously nonstop. I thought I should let this butterfly fly out. As I gently opened the window, without wasting time the butterfly flew away and left me with my happy soul. From afar I blew a kiss and thought, 'Now you can fly as high as you can go, but thank you for making my autumn afternoon so glorious.'

Some people in the evening in autumn like to have good wine and good cheese that makes the life the maturity of the soul. But for me in every season I love to see the beauty of nature so I thought it would be nice to bring my soul to the park and enjoy the autumn evening. In the park I hanged around by the lake and the little clouds ran smoothly by in the peacefully quiet evening but left the sad summer behind. The breeze made my mind calm; I looked at the trees. A dried leaf had fallen and dried grasses died away and became silent in autumn. While I stood by the lake I heard the water lapping with slow sounds by the shore. The earth gave me the gravity to stay on as I looked down at the earth; everything was bright and beautiful. I was very grateful for the opportunity to be on this planet earth and the feeling of joy made me want to cry. I looked up at the heavens, full of excitement; I just can't wait to see the beauty of heaven but time will tell. My eyes wiggled at the autumn sky and my mind talked, saying the sky was so beautiful, full of life. At these moments my spirit, with my gentle voice, whispered about peace.

As the late autumn sun began to set I was so excited to see the spectacular autumn sunset and the beauty of nature. The birds warbled a song then quickly sought their nest. Suddenly the peaceful silence was disturbed with a squawking sound – it was the heron flying over my head, slowly landing by the lake and standing at the waterside. The heron is my favourite and I always watch the single heron every time I come to the park. They're always on their own in the water; their wings flash white and with their long necks I've always found the heron very beautiful. Their open eye show their long leg one leg lifted I thoughts rather sexy but sometime wading without seeming to move. Anyway, the evening autumn sun had goes down while the night was coming with the wind softly blowing and bringing a slight chill to the air. I could see the fish staying still in the water; they could be sleeping. The autumn night started to dance; that was meant to remind me that time was running out and the park would close at any moment now. I left the park with leaves still blowing around off the trees, some going into the pond and floating around, and I left the autumn night, silent on the earth.

The autumn wind at midnight was blowing through my mind, right up to the wet sky, and my whole body drained out, making me be completely without energy. My ears could hear the sound of the autumn rain dropping on the roof while the wind night slapped my window. Stretching my body in bed, I grabbed a small pillow to my chest while my eyes watched the magnificent full moon; without noticing I closed my eyes but could hardly sleep. The sound of the autumn night's rain gave me such a sad night and left me like in pain. This was because my mind was thinking about my mum, which reminded me of her life; the hard times she went through with my father left me really heartbroken. It was so difficult to get out of my mind, thinking about their relationship over and over, and I felt the world surrounding me, full of darkness.

My eyes were fresh and awake and I walked to every corner of my room then slowly pushed open the window – wooops! It was very cold but so fresh and the rain had stopped. I stood for a few minutes enjoying the late-hour autumn air, and in the dark I could see the misty morning. My soul listened to the silence, which was a very peaceful silence, until the birds flew at and shook the bare trees that were reaching up to the foggy sky. I found it to be a very strange bird at this hour – well, it could be anything. My hand started to feel frozen; quickly I shut the window and warmed my hand on the heater then went straight into my cosy bed. The silent late hour in autumn also reminded me of my father like a very bad dream that I could hardly get out of my mind.

I looked at the time; it was two in the morning. My eyes were still awake but I had a small headache thinking how unlucky my mum and myself were in our lives. My heart was on fire, burning like hell, thinking all about my father's character. I grabbed my pillow hard from time to time and tried to control my mind from getting too upset. The autumn night sank deeper and I felt the cold walking on my body. Gently I pulled on the blanket over my chilled feet and all over and lay in silence, listening to the early-hour autumn wind. I loved so much in the early hours of autumn, lying in bed and spending my time bringing back memories of my mum and myself, our unlucky lives. It gave me so much stress, thinking of what we both had been through. I couldn't even make my brain think about other things. During the sleepless night I lay in bed, wide awake, and I could see the autumn leaves fall across my windowpane, like a flying bird in the dark. Again the sleepless night still kept me awake for a long time and I looked up at the autumn's morning skies, greys and blues everywhere. But the sky seemed very clear and there was no sign of rain, which is wonderful at that time of year. And the sleepless night made me lie awake, thinking what a night, having conversations on my own created a very peaceful life, full of joy. My spirit had given me a glowing smile on this autumn morning – another day to continue my life on this planet earth.

Winter Walk of Life

It was November 1; the winter season had begun, which is my favourite season after spring but you had no idea how long it would stay in your life. The first reason I love winter is because I cover up my whole body and keep my skin fair; I love very much to see my skin becoming whiter. I'm sure people over here think that I am mad because almost every single person in London is crazy about the sun so their skin can get tanned. But not me and not the people in Malaysia, especially for the men, because for them women with white skin are prettier. That's why I never married a Malaysia man because with the brown colour of my skin they think I am ugly. Well, nothing much I can do about it but I am so happy to stay in London because they love my skin and they pay for sunbeds to become brown. Forget about skin; what is most important is that I am very happy with my boy in my life. That's all I want. My son Ryan makes my life grow again and day by day brings happiness to my life that I've never had before.

Anyway, winter is the season when the whole world seems to go to sleep. In the season of winter the weather gets very cold every day and the ground is asleep; the trees and plants seem to be dead. The cold doesn't bother me at all; in fact I love it very much because it seems I can sleep forever. And winter is the best season for having a treat because of the cold; for example, sitting at home having a nap because it is too cold. And to warm up the body you have hot chocolate or wine. But what makes me so depressed is rain, rain, rain, and the freezing cold that makes my life so miserable. Well, that is the nature of life, and I've lived in this country long enough for me to understand about the weather, and now the winter had arrived. But sometimes the winter comes without warning, all a of sudden the snow dropping and covering everything like a white blanket. Again I should know that this is the British weather so nothing should surprise me.

I felt the year was passing so quick; the summer had gone completely but it seemed like only yesterday and now without realising winter had arrived with a new chapter in life. I started to put my summer clothes away and bring out my winter clothes, especially as London is the city of fashion and beauty and lifestyle. I just can't wait to wear winter clothes because my skin would be completely covered up for six months then I am very happy for next summer to exploit my fair skin. I love to wear my favourite long black coat that touches the floor and stops me from shivering. This nice coat gives my body so much warmth and holds tight to my skin with loving beauty. I love to wear a hat in winter to hold my long black hair very tidily and to keep my brain warm all the time. Every time when I go out I make sure that my hat is on my head and sits very proudly as a British which I love it. As it's wintertime, to keep my feet warm obviously I have to wear boots; honestly I hate to wear boots and socks but I'm left with no choice. I have a few pairs of boots but only one particular pair that I wear to go everywhere, even to the park. Because it's winter, sometimes the park is full of mud and those boots will be with me through the mud until I'm back home. I thoughts, boot very proud than the normal shoe because it take us through very challenging journey and safely to the end.

Anyway, winter in London sometimes can be freezing with the temperature dropping to zero and with tumbling snow. Especially when the rain falls down it becomes even more cold and the trees seem like they've died; nothing ever grows. If the weather is too cold I prefer to stay indoors and enjoy a cup of hot chocolate with full-fat milk and sit near the heater while watching *Deal or No Deal* or *Antiques Roadshow* – these are my favourite programmes. But sometimes I think that when the season of winter arrives I feel like I've been given a secret message and brought a story. And that winter story is for me to share with someone in my life but never tell them what exactly is in my heart. In life I still have to learn how to fall in love in the natural beauty of winter. But my soul always whispers that the freezing winter would give me big warm hugs full of love because the white winter is waiting for me.

On Sunday morning I wanted to get up early but the weather was so cold and the magical, sweet, tender voice begged me to hug him. My prince Ryan is a big boy but he's still like a little baby so I grabbed his body close to me, with my arm around him, warming him up, and gave him a gentle kiss on his warm, sweet face but he was still soundly asleep. Slowly I exhaled and let him enjoy his sleep in a warm blanket and inhaled slowly as I walked down from the bed. Slowly I tiptoed to the window; as soon as I opened the blinds I could see a blanket of snow covering the green grass in my garden; surely the snow had fallen silently overnight. It was sunny everywhere and I stood for a few minutes looking at the snowflakes being thrown around in the air and landing on the ground. I had a smile on my face welcoming the new winter morning. I love snow and to be outside on a snow day makes it just the best day of my life and I could not miss a single minute of it.

Every Sunday I feel like life is very simple and Sunday is the day for me to be free from everything. Whoop! I could feel the cool beginning to run in my blood and my bare feet were freezing like they were ice-cold but it didn't stop me from going out to meet the snow. As the sun was shining, brightening everything and slowly rising between the trees, I thought, 'On this bright Sunday in winter one of the pleasurable treats for me is to enjoy the snow. It's not often that we have snow in London so I won't miss a single minute of it.' Slowly I tidied up my bed but tried not to wake my little boy Ryan, who was sleeping like a prince. Quickly I got ready before the snow stopped dropping and wore woollen socks to keep my feet completely warm then I was ready to have a fun time. As soon as I was out from the front door – whoop! The cold just sparkled in my face; it was so chilly but I felt I was awake and had been brought to the new world of a winter day. Happily I walked everywhere as long as there was snow; it just brought warmth to my soul and the cold nipped at my nose. The morning air was lovely, with the wind promising another day and another life and plenty of winter days.

I decided to go to the park because that was the place to play with snow. As soon as I entered the park I couldn't describe how sensational it was to see the whole entire park covered with snow; it was the most beautiful natural creation. A lot of people were taking advantage, enjoying the snow with family, the couples were especially that the children were happily playing – surely the school had cancelled classes. So exciting – quickly I grasped small clumps of snow, throwing them away, and kept repeating this a few times. At the same time I could feel my breath inside of me was glowing and filling me with wholly. Then I started to walk around the park to see the beautiful snow on the ground suddenly my feet drop deep in the snow it makes me so flattering. I then stood in front of the lakes; it was amazing to see the lake covered in ice. I felt like putting my feet on the frozen lake and walking freely to heaven, glowing; obviously I couldn't do that because the ice was not hard enough. So I continued my walk while watching the pretty snowflakes falling from the sky, silently covering on the branches, full of frost, then everything was covered. I just let the wind blow in my direction so I could feel the soft, tender snowflakes falling on my face and giving me a kiss on my cheek. But sadly the unique white snow didn't stay on me for long. As soon as I blinked my eyes it melted away. No doubt I was surrounded by others, people full of noise and screaming, throwing the snow at each other. The air was dead but when I looked up the sky was white; look like the sky makes my future purity of love and clean like a snow. Gosh, my hands were freezing cold but I still could not get enough of the snow. Suddenly I could hear leaves whispering, saying that was enough for today; tomorrow would be another day. My eyes kept blinking, enjoying the depiction of beauty that I had seen. Oh dear, I could feel my lips get hard and cracked as soon as I bit it so I walked away and left the winter breath with the snow covering the whole park like a clean white shirt. With a smile I thought, 'What a marvellous time I've had on my own.'

Sitting in my living room I was thinking what I was going to have for lunch as winter leaves me hungry most of the time. Soup in the winter is perfect and reminded me of my mother's chicken soup; no one makes soup like she did, so very beautifully delicious. Well, I can't cook like my mum so I decided to have vegetable soup at my favourite café on the high street. My heart becomes very cheerful as soon as my brain thinks about food. The midday sun still shines but in winter the sun goes down in the early afternoon and soon would set. All of a sudden the sky got sad and the grey clouds started to cry so I'd better go out now before it was too late. I rushed myself to get ready and as soon as I opened the front door suddenly rain came out of the air together with snowflakes – well, this is the city of London, it didn't surprise me at all. Luckily I had a hat on my head so I just walked in the rain like people in London do without an umbrella. I like rain, especially the winter rain – it gives my life so much glory.

Anyway, it took me more or less ten minutes to get to the café on high street – thank God they had my vegetable soup. There was an empty seat in the corner by the window; quickly I took that table before somebody could get it. It was the perfect spot so I could watch the people walking past while enjoying vegetable soup with French bread. After eating I love to give my stomach a rest and looked at the people running around, rushing on their journeys in the cold, wet winter. All those busy lives put a smile in my heart, and their characters make my day happy; it was very interesting.

Suddenly I saw a man with a dirty face and naked feet; with one foot he was shuffling, crossing the road. I just looked at him, wondering where he was going but as he came closer his face looked very sad. He stopped at the rubbish bin right in front of me then his hand started searching in the bin – ummm… he was homeless. But I carefully watched what he was trying to find in the bin, then I saw that one by one he collected cigarette butts. He wore a light blue T-shirt full of stains, and had an untidy face and white dirty blanket in his hand. But luckily it was raining so the rain washed his greasy hair and it dried by itself. He then sat on the floor with his blanket on his lap and looked straight at me. Quickly I pretended to look at something then I thought his body must be very smelly; luckily I was inside the café. He brought out a lighter from his pocket and lit one of the cigarette butts that he'd collected in the bin and smoked it to the end. He had a few cigarette butts and he finished them all. I could see his body was a bit shaky – it looked like he had some addiction. Slowly he outstretched his arms and started to beg for some money from every single person that walked past. I'd been sitting in the café for about forty-five minutes since he'd arrived and he hadn't got any money yet. I am sure people hate to give money to them because most tramps are drug addicts and have drinking problems. My heart felt sorry when I looked at him all alone touching his dry face from wind exposure but that is his best choice; nothing much people can do about it. I know they have issues, problems with drugs and alcohol, but I always give some money to homeless people anywhere I see them. Because I don't know what they've been through in life; also the way they look makes me feel sorry for them and makes me feel guilty if I don't give something. Especially when I do my shopping at Tesco or M&S – there's always a beggar in front of the main entrance. Well, I guess this is how it is to be homeless. Anyway, when I looked at him I could see in his eyes that he was starving and his soul was hurting; at the same time I wondered where he was going to lay his head during the night. I wished I could stop my heart from thinking about him, but this is me; I can't help myself. It was time for me to make a move and on my way out I stood in front of him and dropped in his arms a £5 note. He looked up at me, his eyes shining, and with a smile he said, 'That is exactly what I want.'

I smiled back and left him with the £5 note; suddenly I heard him call out, 'God bless.'

I stopped, turned around and looked at him; with a smile I put my right hand to the left of my chest and my heart whispered, 'God bless you too.'

The afternoon had gone and the winter rain had stopped but the evening winter wind started to blow and brought a breeze to the evening life. I changed my winter day clothes and put on a purple velvet evening winter dress. I walked in a circle round in the living room while my mind talked to my soul, which put a smile in my heart. My eyes looked at my surroundings and gently my heart whisper, wish my house in the countryside especially during the night can enjoying insect winter screaming like a music while my body relaxing. Seated by the fire with a glass of red wine, listening to the winter winds whisper. Being with a loved one sitting under the full moon while watching the stars flicker one by one. Cuddled up in the chilling winter cold, hearing leaves and flowers falling on the ground and watching the snow fall on the ground. This kind of life would always be inside me and remind me of when I was a little girl growing up in the countryside, and that is where I belong, except the weather. Even though that time had passed and been gone for a long time it was still fresh in my mind and would never die. Anyway, sitting on the sofa with my prince Ryan beside me, together we started a tiny song with a words, 'Hug me now, kiss me now, I don't want to live without you, nothing's gonna change my love for you.'

My prince Ryan loves this song and he will sing this song to me before going to bed; it makes me over the moon and I am a very happy mum in the world. I looked outside and the sky was so blue, the colour of a sapphire stone without a ring; it made me whisper to my prince Ryan three precious words: 'I love you.' He looked at me with his pink cheeks and his glorious smile, so pure and true, then he replied, 'I love you too, you are my life and you are my sunshine.'

To hear those astonishing words, I was in heaven; the evening winter was calm and my soul was over the moon. The happiness that he gives me – there is nothing more that I can ask for in this world. His beautiful eyes looked at me with so much meaning; gently I asked him, 'Why do you look at me like that?'

He gave me such a cheeky smile which made me to kiss him over and over. He looked at me and replied, 'Mummy! You are so pretty.'

He is such an adorable diamond; my heart melted away, then I said, 'Aaaaa… thank you, that is so beautiful and you are my world.'

The evening winter had flown by without me noticing; all of a sudden I could feel that the chilly winter nights had run over my body. I looked at my little prince curled up, his body warm in the blanket and him sucking his thumb in his mouth – so adorable. His sweet, lovely face just made me stare at him for hours and hours – I just wanted to hold him and care for him forever. I gentle kissed his red chubby cheeks and softly ran my fingers through his blond hair. I grabbed my mobile phone and turned it to silent so as not to disturb his sleep, and I could focus on thinking about what was on my mind.

On this winter night there was nothing that I wanted more than concentrating and making a plan of when I could go home to visit my mum's graveyard. On this particularly chilly winter night all I wanted was to be on my own with my little prince without anyone disturbing me. I switched on the light and could see the snow was softly falling down on the ground but the air in my room was still silent which made my winter night very peaceful. I walked towards the window to draw the curtains but I could see the storm covering the skies in darkness and the late gusts kept knocking at my window. There were no stars twinkling in the sky and no moon to brighten the world on the winter night. Suddenly from the lamp-lit streets I could see the poor homeless man wandering around in the snow. My heart was crying, seeing him in the cold – I just hoped he had a place to warm him for the rest of the night. I could see my window start to fill up with frost and slowly drew the curtain then tried to find a candle. As much as I love winter, sometimes I feel really depressed especially as the darkness arrives much too soon.

During the winter I love to be inside my house surrounded by candles, which warm it up in every corner. So I lit my candle and let the flame be the light which would brighten the winter night. I put on my favourite CD piano music, especially 'Fur Elise' by Beethoven; I can listen to that over and over without getting bored. And I grabbed a glass of Amarone, my favourite Italian red wine, and a few slices of pecorino toscano, my favourite Italian cheese, and sat in the living room. I'm not a drinker but I love to have a glass of red wine; it helps me to unwind at the end of a winter day. I had a sip of wine with every single bite of cheese; it brought delight to my winter night while I watched the candle burning strong. With the piano music playing nonstop, it made my soul fully awake. The wine put a smile on my face and the journey of the winter night started to begin. I watched the candle flicker out of sight and danced, full of joy. The candle burned, bringing colours, yellow, blue and white – it just made my heart melt with love throughout the night. To see the candle burning, it makes my life be full of light, forever bright, while the winter air whispers of the magic of love. The good wine goes smoothly with the good cheese and I started to feel a little tipsy, but my mind was full of a smile. I stretched my legs, making myself comfortable, and took the last bite of cheese; it melted in my mouth and the taste was divine, full of protein.

The winter night slowly went past and the candle started to get smaller; it gave me a warning that it was time for bed. The night brings dewfall and I tried to open my eyes wider to look at the wall clock; the time showed exactly midnight. The winter midnight was getting very cold; my bare feet started to get freezing and my lips were like ice. I spoke from my heart with a few words in the dark but there was no one around to share them with me; only my soul comforted my sadness. To think about the about my late mum now one or twice I get hurt and emotional but in a world full of craziness at that moment. My eyes looked at the window, the glass was blurry, with the white winter's breath whispering to find peace. Before going to bed I took the last shot to empty my glass and I felt the winter midnight brought me happiness as a mother to my prince Ryan.

Slowly I walked to my room and as soon as I entered the room I saw my Prince Ryan peacefully asleep like an angel just sent to earth from heaven. It put a smile on my face and all my sleepiness, tiredness and sadness disappeared because he was so perfect and so beautiful. I came closer, wanting to kiss him goodnight but my movement woke him up. I thought, 'Oops! Sorry, I didn't mean to disturb you.' I took him, with his drowsy eyes, and he went back to sleep, thank God. I kept looking at his adorable face and I still couldn't believe that he'd entered into my life and was going to be with me forever. It reminded me of the day he was first in my arms; I cried floods of tears. It was very emotional and overwhelming – no words can describe how beautiful life is. Only my cheerful soul whispered to my heart that this little angel is a miracle and his little warm smile shines through my whole life. In this winter midnight with my Prince Ryan in my life so hard believe but he makes my life happy ending.

Flying Home, Visiting My Mum's Graveyard

20th December 2022, I was on the blue sky flying back home through the mountains of clouds at last. Soon my flight home had begun but from now I only hold tightly within my heart and there remind until I see in my own eyes my graveyard. But flying back this time, I had so much sadness and tears fell upon my cheeks knowing my mum was not there waiting for me anymore. When the plane took to the runway to depart, straight away I felt my heart tearing apart and memories stabbing my heart like broken glass. Sitting by the window looking at the blue sky and at the rosy clouds and the setting sun, it made me sad. But then slowly I looked down upon the earth thinking my mum was waiting for me. Seeing all of its glory, however, somewhere deep inside me my heart had become a wound spreading pain. I could see there would be no shining, no happiness and no home sweet home when I arrived at my mum's home. But the magnificent sun burst with a smile brighter than the skies to guide my way home and I hoped the angels would guide me to the other side of the world.

The plane started to fly high but my body and my whole system went lower; please God, lift me up, I want to be at my mum's home happy and peaceful. I wished I had wing so I could spread them and soar high towards the sky and fly underneath the clouds and make a fast landing on the ground to be at my mum's graveyard. Suddenly I felt the cool breeze in my face like the touch of an angel which meant my mum's soul was waiting for me – just a wonderful feeling. This feeling took my breath away and the breathtaking view of the sky made me think I was not very far from where she was in heaven. While flying high in the sky most of the time I prayed to be brought safely down to the earth to peacefully visit my mum's graveyard. Knowing this time my mum was not there for me, I felt so very sad and lost, especially as I could still see my mum's fresh smile; it just made my knees so weak. This time I didn't sleep much on the plane, just sat in silence, feeling lots of pain, but there were particles of pain I felt deep inside me while watching the clouds. I wished I could blow it away towards the crying sky and let it join the wind and let the pain fly high as mountain. However, with my son Ryan and my partner Giovanni looking at me I tried to smile so they couldn't see the hurt. In silence I watched my son Ryan, seven years old, behave cheekily. I laughed nonstop, which made my tears pour down, and I felt I hold the pain.

After thirteen hours of flying, I came back to the earth and landed on dry ground to feel the humidity and see the beauty of greenery everywhere; it took my breath away. As soon as my eyes looked at the ground from the window I felt so relieved and thanked God for bringing me to the earth; it was a perfect landing.

Arriving in Malaysia in late afternoon, then I had to take another flight to my mum's city, which would take another few hours, and of course it would be too late and I would be too tired to visit my mum's graveyard. But the next day I woke up early and ready to instead to her house but straight to her permanent home. I was so much looking forward to seeing her where she lay in peace. On my way to my mum's graveyard, I felt lost in the world, all empty inside, and like there was nothing left, just thinking about my mum lying in the wet clay. It was still fresh in my mind and I always remembered the moment I received the news that my mum had died; my heart was torn in two, one side filled with heartache and the other dying with her. And the day my mum died she lay alone in the room; sadly everyone couldn't be with her which left her in silence. On my side a thousand miles away during the early hours just after my prayer, standing by the window and looking at the sky, I couldn't help but nod. I am sure that that day my mum had to leave me and others when her life on earth was through, and I trust that God has better plans for her. Since my mum's gone I've often dreamed of her in the middle of the night when the world is fast asleep. In my dreams my mum comes with her beautiful smile and doesn't talk much then disappears, but I hold her tightly within my heart, which reminds me that we will meet again. And every morning when I open my eyes, I know that my mum will never come back and my heart still aches with sadness and secret tears will flow.

Flying Home, Visiting My Mum's Graveyard

This is what it means to lose a precious person which no one will ever know.

I had arrived at my destination, but of course I had to park the car and walk to find my mum's graveyard. As Malaysia is a hot country, walking to my mum's graveyard I started to feel the heat, but as I was born in this country, the heat was in my heart. With every step I took I felt my body so broken and tears started to fall in my heart because I never expected to come to see her where she'd been buried. Slowly walking down the alleyway, some mud accompanied me, my son Ryan and my partner Giovanni. To walk to my mum's graveyard was the hardest thing in my entire life and I felt my soul in this world was lost slowly as I whispered, 'Please help me be strong.' The sun burst strong; there was hardly any wind and the heat start to climb in my body, but I didn't feel the heat anymore because I had a broken dream, a broken wing and a broken heart.

It was so easy to find my mum's grave right in front of the gate. I soon entered, but my mind, my eyes, everything became blurry. Here I was flying a thousand miles away, finally sitting in front of my mum's grave. Slowly touching the gravestone, I closed my eyes and with my heart whispered, 'Mum, I am here for you but sorry I'm a little late.' My eyes looked at the gravestone with my mum's name written on it. Suddenly my thoughts were running crazily through my mind but I prayed that God would give me strength, then I wrote my mum's name in my heart where it would stay forever. Slowly I was on my knees reading and praying for her to tell God take my mum's soul to heaven and rest in peace.

After finishing reading a prayer for my mum I took my own moment to be with her then my eyes gently looked up at the open sky, feeling that the earth was keeping on spinning. But I kept my silence in my world without noticing warm tears running down like a river. I felt so much heartbreak thinking that my mum was lying asleep, all alone; I wished I could see her one more time and hear her last voice. At that moment I felt life was following a path and my world was not the same after my mum had walked away and left me without saying goodbye. It broke my heart into pieces to lose my mum and slowly I whispered to her spirit, 'Mum, you didn't go alone; a part of me went with you.'

Sitting beside my mum's grave, I wanted so much to hug her but only tears dropped left a puddle with a memory. And thinking of those special memories of us would always bring a smile for me. If only I could have my mum back for just a little while, then we could sit and talk again just like we used to do. The fact that my mum was here would always cause me pain but my mum is forever in my heart until I meet her again. But I always remember from before that my mum was a beautiful woman and I always know her life from start to end. And I am so glad that I was her daughter and to know her as a mother and as a friend. I am so lucky and blessed to have all those many years with my mum and with her love my soul is at rest; there is no need for tears. I have only one mother in the whole wide world, so in my mind I was still thinking that my mum is not dead; she was still waiting for me as she promised. But now, sitting in front of my mum's grave,

Flying Home, Visiting My Mum's Graveyard

I could feel life had already separated us forever. However, I knew it was only my mum's soul saying goodbye to her body, but her spirit would be with me always. I wished my mum could feel the suffering I felt the day God took her last breath; I was lost in the dark and my world was collapsing, and the thought of not seeing her again and the hurt, the pain, I can't describe. My heart was bleeding badly. Since the day my mum had to go, every time I think of her my heart has been left broken, but the memories were shining brightly within this broken heart, in the tears that still flowed.

I was at my mum's grave every day for eight days, praying and talking to her soul, but for the last day my heart cried and it was painfully hard to say goodbye. I took my precious time, whispering to my mum's spirit, 'Mum, you are my first love and I know even if I said a thousand words I could not bring you back because you are gone forever from this world. And I also know that even if I cried a thousand tears, still I could not bring you back because you are in heaven far away from me. Although I'm sad, I'm happy at the same time because your soul is resting in peace and your body is free from pain. I know we can't see each other anymore but you are safe inside my heart, and that's where you'll always be.' I gently closed my eyes, thinking my mum would be up in heaven because God only takes the best. But for now, goodbye, my lullaby, my soul. I really miss you, Mum, you are my world and losing you was the hardest thing in my life – be back again soon.'

Acknowledgements

To my brothers, Ridzwan and Zambri, thank you for your hard work looking after our mum day and night, which I never repaid. I can't imagine how difficult it was for you both to go through that, especially Ridzwan, who had a hard time with cancer. I know this is a difficult time for him and the pain is huge, but I never stop kneel down and count my blessing for him. With the cancer his life started to get hard, but he is a fighter and went on with his life, with his soul journey to walk upon. Sadly, his life was taken for granted; after his cancer cleared his body continued with another problem, which was kidney stones and a swollen heart. This was not good for him. My brother Ridzwan is a very strong and intelligent person, accepting everything with calmness and bravery, keeping things under control. Honestly, he is an incredible person and very stubborn too. I feel so sorry for him but there is nothing much I can do; however, he's always in my prayers.

And Zambri too has had a hard time with his marriage while he was busy looking after my mum, and this was the time his wife asked for the divorce. He really had a rough week before my mum died; life was so hard for him, juggling work, my mum and his marriage. There were so many things he had to handle, but he really stayed strong in that tough time – I'm so proud of him. I felt so sorry for him, with his life struggling along with the hustle and bustle. At last, he accepted what his wife wanted, which was a divorce – finally the marriage was over just a few days before our mum passed away. His ex-wife made his life so complicated at that time, but his heart was so strong; he continued life with a broken heart. He asked himself, why did things have to be this way? Why had life put him in that tough situation? So many things in his head but then he accepted there are always lessons in life to be learned. So now he is happy and free, flying his wings, away all the pressure that he had with his wife, and making his world a better place.

For my little sister Nurul, I am beyond lucky to have a gifted sister like you. As a single mother with four children, I can't imagine how hard life has been for you. But you are always there to play your thoughtful part and you are there when everyone needs you, so I am so proud of you. Thank you for everything that you did for our mum.

Of course, I will never forget the name of Giovanni; he is my rock and he is one of the special people who makes my world a better place. He always does the best for me in life and he is there to lend a hand before I ask for anything and he never wants anything in return. If anything upsets me he will be truly concerned and I can't thank him enough for all the things he has done, especially as he really cared about my mum's condition – it means the world to me.

He is the one who's by my side when no one else is there and he always helps me through the tough times because I always count on him. It's a true blessing that I have such a loving, down-to-earth partner to lean on during times when nobody else listens, but he'll lend me an ear. He is more than my life partner; he has a special place in my heart. That's why he is my best friend because he gives me a helping hand and shoulder to lean on. Since the day he entered my life he's made me better and better – a million thank-yous.

Lastly, my lovely cousin Kamal; I'm always on the phone with him because we're so close. He's like my little brother, especially as our mums are sisters. My cousin is like my best friend; he is very honest and loyal, so of course he is someone I can trust. I ask him to do many things for me and he never says no and is there to help me. Sometimes he can be annoying but even then he's always there for me. The most beautiful thing about him is that he always listens to my advice on anything. He is the person who is there when I need a shoulder to cry on and someone to laugh with. We may be apart but he always stays close to my heart. Especially as every week he drove his motorbike for more than an hour to see my mum and deliver the news about my mum to me. So here I just want to let him know that he means the world to me, and thank you for all you have done for me.

As for myself, life is about accepting the challenges along the way and choosing to keep moving forward with happiness and sadness in my journey. Every problem that is given to me I accept with an open heart, and I try to settle then go on with life. At times the journey gets too difficult and I'm plagued with too many uncertainties, but I still never give up. I keep my life alive which no one know what I been through because I know soon the tides will turn and a new ray of sunshine is born.

Thank you to my brothers Ridzwan and Zambri, and my sister Nurul for always updating me about our mum's condition, giving me strength to believe in a miracle. I'm so proud of the patience and understanding the three of you had with our mum. I only wish you three could look inside my heart and see how sad I was. I always think of the times the three of you were there for our mum and doing the best for her. Well, those times give me so much hurt and pain because I could only hear what mum went through, but I couldn't be there to help. Life has a way of tearing me down but the three of you have been there to encourage me and keep me strong enough to continue with life. The three of you helped our mum face her fears to climb higher in her life than she ever cared to go because you all wanted our mum to recover and go back to her normal life. For the three of you to look after our mum meant the world to me.

Thank you to Giovanni for caring for me through all the years when I was so down, worried about my mum. And lastly thank you to my cousin Kamal, who always talked to me and gave me so much confidence in everything.

I just want to let all of you know that you all mean the world to me; even though I might not say it, I appreciate all of you. I feel blessed to have all of you in my life.